ESSAYS ON POSTMODERNISM AND SOCIAL WORK

edited by
ADRIENNE S. CHAMBON
ALLAN IRVING

Canadian Scholars' Press Inc.   Toronto   1994

Essays on Postmodernism and Social Work

First published in 1994 by
Canadian Scholars' Press Inc.
180 Bloor St. W., Ste. 402,
Toronto, Ontario   M5S 2V6

Canadian Cataloguing in Publication Data

Main entry under title:

Essays on postmodernism and social work

ISBN   1-55130-051-6

1. Social service – Philosophy. 2. Postmodernism –
Social aspects. I. Chambon, Adrienne S., 1949 –
II. Irving, Allan.

HV40. E77 1994   361.3'01   C94–931652–0

Page layout and cover design by Brad Horning

Printed and bound in Canada

TABLE OF CONTENTS

INTRODUCTION   1

CHAPTER 1   3
THE THERAPEUTIC IDEA IN CONTEMPORARY SOCIETY
LAURA EPSTEIN

CHAPTER 2   19
FROM IMAGE TO SIMULACRA: THE MODERN/POSTMODERN
DIVIDE AND SOCIAL WORK
ALLAN IRVING

CHAPTER 3   33
FEMINIST POSTMODERNISM AND THE CHALLENGE OF DIVERSITY
CATRINA BROWN

CHAPTER 4   47
BORROWED KNOWLEDGE IN SOCIAL WORK: AN INTRODUCTION
TO POST-STRUCTURALISM AND POSTMODERNITY
LINDSAY H. JOHN

CHAPTER 5   61
POSTMODERNITY AND SOCIAL WORK DISCOURSE(S):
NOTES ON THE CHANGING LANGUAGE OF A PROFESSION
ADRIENNE S. CHAMBON

INTRODUCTION

More and more in recent years the word postmodernism has come to inhabit the discourse of the humanities and social sciences. Social work as a field and discipline is no exception. In order to explore the impact of postmodern ideas on social work, a workshop organized by Ph.D. students — Catrina Brown and Lindsay John — and two members of the teaching staff — Adrienne Chambon and Allan Irving — was held at the Faculty of Social Work at the University of Toronto on March 10, 1993. The intention was to provide a stimulating, provocative and timely debate on social work as a profession in the late twentieth century. The five essays in this collection are the revised papers presented at the workshop including the fine keynote lecture by Professor Laura Epstein who taught for many years at the School of Social Service Administration at the University of Chicago.

Laura Epstein challenges us to re-examine the purview and influence of social work, and no longer perceive it as a minor genre or semi-profession, but instead as the dominant field, which has vigorously promoted the therapeutic idea, legitimizing the venue of "therapeutism" in every corner of our lives. She eloquently argues that the mission of social work is founded upon the three core notions of "care, protection and treatment," and promoted through a particular blend of female care-taking features and male tutelary concepts. Taking a historical and Foucaldian reading of our discipline, she leads us to re-examine the mandate of social work as the "construction of character and personhood in capitalist society," making apparent its function of social control, and our contribution, as social workers, to this caring-tutelary vision.

Allan Irving sets out some of the meanings of postmodernism as a term that describes the flux and uncertainty of late twentieth century life, an era of vanished transcendent truths. The transition from modernity to postmodernity is discussed and the ways in which this has altered our sense of the world. Social work, as one of the cultural and social artifacts of eighteenth century Enlightenment thinking, it is suggested, may need to relocate itself within the new reality of postmodernism. The basic question raised in the paper lies at the centre of the modern\postmodern debate: Is the Enlightenment project, as Jurgen Habermas calls it, dead or can it be resuscitated?

Catrina Brown places us in front of a stimulating and fundamental dilemma as she reflects upon the tension between diversity and inclusion which confronts the politics of identity and political mobilisation in the context of postmodern feminism. A feminist postmodern approach to knowledge, by rejecting the essentializing of the feminine location and advocating the plurality of women's experiences, weakens the relevance of identity politics. This move raises questions as to what can be defined as authoritative voices for change, or who is entitled to speak about what. To grapple with these choices, she urges us to re-examine our understanding of identity, and to derive implications for developing an emancipatory social work, its epistemology and, concurrently, a critical pedagogy.

Lindsay H. John invites us to explore the epistemological implications of borrowed knowledge. The adoption of the central tenets of post-structuralist theory in social work revolutionizes our approach to knowledge — from its credulous stance towards metanarratives, to its critique of a humanist subject and the belief in the origin of meaning as located inside individuals. These ideas imply that social work revisit categorically organized representational knowledge and explanatory theories (such as psychopathological explanatory schemas of personality), and alternatively view clients as subjects constituted through a shared knowledge process, encouraging a continuous examination of the discursive logic of our practices.

Adrienne S. Chambon examines critically a number of current practices of discourse in our discipline. She argues that the postmodern text has already infused the field of social work to a considerable extent. Social work has adopted this stance without taking a critical look at the implications. Specifically, the terminology used in social work has greatly evolved over time and is restructuring the meaning of social work practice. The current imagery and textual practices replicate and accentuate the fragmentary, mediatic, electronically cool conception of clients and workers, and a perspective on knowledge as an ever-extending set of contained and revolving products. In this light, social work's expertise is questionably seen as heteronomously defined. She argues in favour of a restructuration of plurality and alternative conceptions through reflexivity.

We would like to thank the former dean of the Faculty, Professor Heather Munroe-Blum who enthusiastically supported our wish to hold such an event and who generously provided funding; and the current acting dean of the Faculty, Professor Marion Bogo who so willingly agreed to provide funds towards publication of the papers. We would like to thank Brad Lambertus, editor at Canadian Scholars' Press, for his fine editorial suggestions; his help and interest have resulted in a much improved manuscript.

CHAPTER 1

THE THERAPEUTIC IDEA IN CONTEMPORARY SOCIETY

LAURA EPSTEIN

INTRODUCTION

In this century we have witnessed the unfolding of an intricate and dominating discourse — "therapeutism" — that has penetrated society (Berger, 1977). We are to the point where the Therapeutic Idea is the preponderant influence on the composition of normative standards for how we conduct ourselves, how we judge people, how we decide with whom to get involved, whom to avoid, where we take a job, bring up children, deal with illness, our bodies, our minds, all our social relations. This is the case throughout the industrialized world; but particularly and most extensively, we in North America live by the Therapeutic Idea. It is one of the four great governing faiths of modernism: psychoanalysis, capitalism, Marxism and democracy.

What does the Therapeutic Idea signify for life in the 90s and beyond? The 1980s were a powerful transitional period. We lived through a decade of unparalleled historical turmoil and change. There were historical transformations and upheavals as significant as the era of democratic revolutions in the late eighteenth century, the events of 1848 or the events of 1968 (Best and Kelner, 1991). These changes show no signs of letting up. It is no surprise that philosophers and social critics developed postmodern theories to try to understand what is going on.

The Big Story is that we are taking part in changes that make us question prevailing social theories and policies. Capitalism is being restructured and transformed, not by way of any left-wing design, but by virtue of working out of its own processes. Postmodernism is one of the intellectual trends for dealing with new and emerging issues. Postmodern theorists do not offer broad and comprehensive explanations. They avoid broad theories, arguing that comprehensive theories are "totalizing" and "universalistic," if not "utopian."

Postmodernist thinkers, however, are superb micro-analysts. Michel Foucault is the postmodern philosopher and historian of ideas who has dealt directly and extensively with the nature of the human sciences. His work puts an irreversible shape on contemporary thinking about the development of therapeutic ideas and the nature of the power incorporated in the theories and practices of therapeutic institutions (see Foucault, 1979; also, Dreyfus and Rabinow, 1982: 143–167). Foucault's themes fit with the motifs pursued by sociological scholars such as Reiff, London and Halmos. They augment Kuhn's analysis of the nature of scientific development. They form a context for understanding Grunbaum's critique of the scientific and epidemiological grounding of psychoanalysis (Grunbaum, 1984; Halmos, 1970; Kuhn, 1970; London, 1964; Reiff, 1968).

WHY THE PRE-EMINENCE OF THE THERAPEUTIC IDEA?

Therapeutic ideas have come to be considered transhistorical, scientifically objective, apolitical — good for you, healthy. Freudianism is the original source of therapeutics. The philosophical core of the Therapeutic Idea is a set of interlocking beliefs, values, commitments and commandments based on original Freudianism and, to some extent, on its alterations that have introduced variation and complexity into the belief system.

The core Freudian ideas set forth that there is a universal human nature with regularly existing, lawful characteristics. The "dynamics" of personal behaviour, meaning how people function, intra-psychically and in interpersonal relationships, supposedly follows rules asserted to have been discovered by Freud and his disciples in the course of treating patients. The theory holds that unconscious conflicts strongly determine thoughts, feelings and behaviour; that early childhood experiences influence development in the world and establish the order of one's life; and that control of our destiny can be achieved by emphasizing our independent strivings and abilities. Psychoanalysis is put forward as a means of alleviating distress as we strain and falter in attempting to carry out our destiny and the rules of living.

There was something about the early part of the twentieth century, when psychoanalytic doctrine was first developed, that lent itself to a celebration of psychoanalytic ideas. Freud himself disseminated his psychoanalytic ideas to the study of literature, and he produced a body of narratives offered as case studies. Freud used literary images to stand for supposedly real "structures" of the mind. For example, he transformed the high drama of *Oedipus Rex* into the symbolic Oedipus complex, a mundane family problem that he and his followers glorified. Surrealists led the movement to put psychoanalytic ideas into art and literature, and these ideas spread widely in the arts and the media.

Making the turn from the nineteenth century, the world entered the era of burgeoning science, exploration and experimentation. Psychoanalysis, the airplane, the Bolshevik revolution, the American Red Scare and space travel came into being. As psychoanalysis established itself, the doctrine deeply influenced the manner in which people perceived of and dealt with their lives and well-being. It shaped modern perceptions, speech and behaviour. Psychoanalysis became a major explanation of our inner life and of the manner in which we deal with our environment.

The Therapeutic Idea is serious business. It is not a peripheral enterprise. Its substance, its implications and its uses in the life of society have raised, and continue to raise, problematic issues. For instance, how are we to explain the simplification and popularization that has been the fate of psychoanalysis; its being turned into a commodity, into an instrument of social policy? And its ability to transcend mutilation, vulgarization, argumentation, misrepresentation and revisionism? How are we to explain the resilience of psychoanalytic theory and the way it travels across countries and disciplines, appearing everywhere and in a multitude of forms and variations? How explain its sturdy expansion in the face of accumulating evidence that its therapies do not work particularly well, even that, some say, "its ineptitude is starkly evident?" (Polsky, 1991). For the practitioners, sponsors and clients of therapeutics, these questions raise issues about the propriety of doing, taking and underwriting therapy.

THE THERAPEUTIC IDEA: ITS NATURE AND FUNCTIONS

The Therapeutic Idea is the foremost non-religious doctrine about how to live in the twentieth century. The Therapeutic Idea analyzes the modern experience of the self. It gives an explanation that has developed into a consensus about what is going on around us and inside us. It suggests what may be the sources of our ill-being and how we are to be consoled for the misery of living. It tells us how to pursue personal growth and self-actualization, or well-being. All this in the context of Western culture, especially but not exclusively in North America. Although the Therapeutic Idea derives primarily from the foundation of Freudianist psychoanalysis and its revisions, it takes different forms in the hands of a variety of authors and specialists. In our times, therapeutism is our guide to the perplexities of modern living.

Psychotherapy is the Therapeutic Idea formed into technologies of the self, that is, individual behaviour changing and mind management. Therapeutic practitioners are those who apply techniques to others. They serve the state and governing elites, doing types of socially constructed work. They classify and arrange the population into categories according to function: for example, students, minimum-wage workers, homeless, addicts, abusers, lay-abouts, schizophrenics and so forth. They administer services to meet human needs revealed and constructed by social processes. They socialize people into occupying appropriate places in the social structure and behaving in the right ways.

Therapeutism is the social movement and the public discourse that collects, arranges and distributes therapeutic ideas. The movement is a two-pronged enterprise; on the one hand it is therapy of individual cases, on the other it is an ideology that explains and shapes present society. The organizations and practices of the therapists of all disciplines combine to form the discourse, and they conduct the movement. The arts, sciences and technologies amplify the effects in a continuous way. Medical psychiatry formally governs the enterprise, and social work provides the foot soldiers and the housekeeping. Psychology does the important research and provides the scientific cachet. In concert with other therapy practitioners, these big three co-ordinate the control, surveillance and tutelage, or the care/protection/treatment, of deviants, disturbers of the political peace and the quietly desperate. Therapists provide the calming, the conflict abatement, the comforting, the education and, where necessary, the guardianship or support of the anxious and bewildered.

This sturdy enterprise cannot and does not function on its own. This is not simply a case of therapeutic entrepreneurs greedily digging in a gold mine of misery and marketing it for self-aggrandizement and profit, although that goes on. The therapeutic enterprise enjoys public and political sanction. It has been dependent on and has collaborated fully with the state, which has been well served by it. It mitigates some of the harshness and horror that can be and often is the lot of many people, both poor and non-poor.

Therapeutism is part of the basic polity of the state. Its role is dissonant, being on the one hand social control, and on the other protector of human rights. The modern American state is a product of the conditions of industrialization and international tensions that emerged with the twentieth century (Dawley, 1991). This state attempted to preserve liberalism and capitalism by imposing restraints on both individuals and on free enterprise. The regulatory state thus emerged as a permanent player both in the market and in private life. State capitalism and the welfare state had arrived. Thereafter there would be

6

continuing tension about the limits and extensions of government intervention in both the market and the lives of citizens. Within this set of state functions, therapeutism grew to be of service in mediating the conflicts that inevitably arose between citizens and the state.

The New Deal ushered in a governing system capable of creating a continuous balancing of corporate dominance and the popular contending forces within American society. Until they lost out under the influence of Reaganism and the globalization of the economy, the American labour movement played an important role in mediating the conflicts among contending interests. This mediating state mechanism, these devices for continuously balancing conflicting interests, became the taken-for-granted American Way. Therapeutism is one of the most important mediating devices available to the state and thus it has become an indispensable feature of governance.

In the United States, the state rules a very large, immensely diverse population. It is distressed by huge pockets of poverty and deviance, by substantial cultural divergence, beset by inability to deal with racism. It has not acquired the welfare state apparatus adequate to deal effectively with its "social questions." Its social welfare, health and education structures have not been adequate to take care of the conflicts that beset modern capitalist societies. The state has, nevertheless, needed to socialize and deter deviance, to fashion a population that can live in relative domestic peace.

The modern state needs non-coercive social control mechanisms. To that end, the state and the therapeutic enterprise have evolved a partnership, sometimes labelled the "therapeutic state." The state-therapy combination creates an immense and complex power that exceeds what therapeutic expertise alone could do. Medical psychiatry provides priestly style, organized influence and a scientific connection. Psychology offers social science and research. Social work stays closely connected to the citizens and delivers the care/protection/ treatment package. Therapeutism is thus our official organ of socialization and benign restraint. It has in reserve the capability of coercion, to be realized through calling on the forces of the judicial and correctional apparatus.

Therapeutism is more than a technology of restraint and socialization. The therapeutic idea in modern society is about the creation and construction of the personal self: the character, values and skills that make one able to succeed in a capitalistic market society where the governing ideology demands that each person be independent economically and psychologically. Many community supports have become thin and weak. They are virtually non-existent among the most socially isolated, the poorest sectors of our citizens (Wilson, 1989). The therapeutic idea has evolved to be a state sanctioned ideology. It is at the heart of our culture. It has developed practices to control the deviant, dangerous and the merely troublesome, and to get self-control and self-actualization for the merely unhappy.

Therapeutism and Social Policy

There is a marked tendency to regard social policies dealing with the whole social system, with general social and problem-solving needs, as being distinctly different from therapeutism. This separateness of the two fields has been made into an enduring conflict within the profession of social work. Other therapeutic practitioners, on the whole, act as if they can ignore the larger social issues, although in actuality they concede the connection, although it is out of their orbit. We argue, however, that the interwoven connections between the macro-social-system and the micro-social-systems are close and indispensable. This argument allows one to try to scrutinize how the minutiae of individual acts and individual practices influence the creation of social policies, and how social policies impinge upon individual acts.

Mature capitalist democracies prefer that social control be non-coercive. This does not mean that coercive means will not be taken, but the sanctions of choice are the remedial, rehabilitative and therapeutic. When social controls are cruel and repressive, the public and the state try to consider them aberrations, even violations of human rights. Certain types of persons who particularly offend the public have been made into exceptions. For example, Americans are willing to maintain capital punishment and long mandatory sentences for selected types of violators who are extremely repugnant in public opinion, for example, violent persons and those in the drug culture. However, the public and the state prefer that, where possible, deviants be medicalized and controlled by therapy.

Therapeutics plays a large role in the socialization and support of all economic classes: the poor, the better-off working-class people and the middle and wealthy classes. All suffer quantities of tension and anxiety, disappointment, bewilderment and despair. It is estimated that one-third of the U. S. population has received therapy from possibly as many as 250,000 psychotherapists of all sorts. Add to this number additional millions aided by the 400,000 persons estimated to be employed as social workers (Lindsey and Kirk, 1992; also Report of the Task Force on Social Work Research, 1991). Social work clients seen in the social agencies of many types, mostly in the public sector, are probably poor and near-poor. These citizens receive interventions in the category of care/protection/ treatment, at the hands of therapeutically trained personnel or those they supervise.[1]

There is a historical relationship between social work and social services for poor people. The modern profession of social work arose in the midst of early twentieth century Progressive Era social movements. These aimed to develop social services to remedy the conditions of the American poor. There was special emphasis on the immigrant poor, who were perceived as social problem bearers because of foreign speech and manners and a tradition of labour unrest that they brought to the United States. Progressives hoped that improvement in the conditions of life and labour of the poor would lead to a decrease in social conflict stemming from problems of inequality. Progressives were searching for ways to intervene in problems of poverty and low wages, especially to mitigate associated problems of alcoholism, wife beating and child neglect. Women, many of whom became prominent in the Progressive movement, expected to have an impact on social problems while creating influential occupations in which to find a respected place (Ehrenreich, 1985; Klein, 1968; Muncy, 1985; Polsky, 1991). There also began a process of organizing a division of labour between influential men and women in the conduct of the developing charity organizations (Katz, 1986, especially pp. 64–66).

The relationship between philanthropy, the medical profession and the poor may antedate the Progressive Era. Castel's recent historical research in France brought to light that the medicalization of poverty came on the scene there at the beginning of the nineteenth century. In the effort to rebuild the society after the French Revolution, philanthropy and the medical profession joined forces to influence the minds and lifestyles of the poor (Castel, 1988).

As Castel interprets the historical record, this alliance between philanthropy and psychiatry came about in France because medical personnel in charge of the asylums acquired credentials as developers of treatment practices targeted at the poor. From there it was a short step to becoming social policy makers. Leaders of asylum reform, such as Phillipe Pinel, broke out of general medicine to start the psychiatric speciality.[2] These people were strongly committed to an Enlightenment outlook, placing high value on science, progress, growth and social engineering. They committed themselves to a social medicine that was a political enterprise. They sought to dominate public health and social hygiene, and to generate the norms for public living habits and morals. These proto-psychiatrists made an alliance with philanthropists who were the proto-social workers. They were interested in developing new techniques for controlling public assistance. Within this perspective, we glimpse the possibility that at least some authorities have been trying to influence the minds of poor people for almost 200 years, believing they might thus reduce the incidence of poverty.

Developments in the United States occurred in a substantially different socio-economic-historical context than post-revolutionary France. Social policy in the United States took a road of developing philanthropic professionalism and bureaucracy. Philanthropists emphasized reform of the moral behaviours of the poor. Organized charity was devising institutional mechanisms for transmitting the values of the city's middle and upper strata downward into the ranks of the poor. The developers of philanthropy emphasized reforming the morals and values of the poor by personal influence. The moral and the medical approaches eventually merged, creating the basis for modern therapeutism (Castel, ibid, p. 101). It appears that early in capitalist development, the poor were diverted from social structural change into attempts to change their minds.

Modern therapeutism has spawned a wide and uneven array of social policies and treatment techniques. Expert power is in place over all economic classes. Social policies have different emphases, depending on whether they are addressed primarily to the poor or the better-off. Therapeutism, however, may be a classless phenomenon. What makes for differences in the way psychotherapy appears — talking and uncovering treatment for the middle-class and psychological thinkers, supportive problem-solving with concrete services for the poor or those poorly endowed with psychological-mindedness — is packaging. Collections of multiple types of intervention are put together in an eclectic mix and dosed out. Who gets what depends on complicated circumstances.

THE PRACTITIONERS

Therapy practitioners, together with the media, are the major purveyors of the Therapeutic Idea. Therapists are crucial players in mapping and outlining the practical activities and beliefs subscribed to by large and important sections of the citizenry. The content of the discourse which therapists create and disseminate, often in loose collaboration with media personages and selected members of the larger public, constitutes theories about the nature of people, explanations of their doings and dealings and suggestions about what they ought to do and think — a moral philosophy of a sort.

Therapy practitioners exist in a web of inter-connected and competitive groups, in several professions and crafts. Each has a somewhat specialized and overlapping habitat. The therapy occupations go by various names: mental health practitioners, clinicians, therapists, or plain professional help, without any specific disciplinary identification.

Medical psychiatry is first among the mental health practitioners; but this was not always the case. Early in the century, the medical world held psychiatry in low esteem. The income of psychiatric practitioners was among the lowest of the specialities. Psychiatry's status strengthened as it achieved better integration into medicine, its psychoanalytic aura taken on to a large extent for embroidery

(Grob, 1983, especially chapter 3, pp. 46–71). It was that decoration, however, which was to form psychiatry's bridge to and its close connection with modern social work. It was the psychoanalytic mystique, carefully maintained, which appealed to novelists and filmmakers as a vehicle for attracting audiences and promoting interest in the apparent deep mysteries of the mind. However, as this century ends, psychiatry is embracing its biological background and tending to relinquish its attachment to a humanistic and increasingly distrusted practice of psychoanalysis.

Clinical psychology has undergone a complicated process of professionalization. It has benefitted through its close association with experimental research. Displaying its doctoral degree as its credential, clinical psychology was able to win identification as "doctor" with a public seemingly in the dark about the distinctions among mental health professionals, a term invented to obscure such distinctions. In spite of disputes with psychiatry over turf, clinical psychology acquired the status of a state licensed occupation. Although keeping its distance, being careful not to become adjunctive psychiatrists, clinical psychology connected itself to the medical male hierarchy, borrowing their authority. Clinical psychology acquired a panache that combined the psychoanalytic terrain with the antiseptic detachment of a scientist. Despite all this, clinical psychology has been unable to establish a firm professional identity and niche (Pallone, 1992: 64–69; VandenBos, Cummings and DeLeon, 1992; also Freedheim, 1992: 725–879).

Pastoral counselling, nursing, occupational therapy, family therapists, family counsellors, marriage counsellors, addiction counsellors, rehabilitation counsellors, street workers, para-professionals and others occupy various roles in the therapeutic panorama. Their status and credentials are complex and sometimes ambiguous, but they are out there "doing therapy." They appear on talk shows, they invite clients through direct mail, they undergo cross-examination on *60 Minutes*.

In this panorama of therapists, social work is a hidden dimension. Social work takes centre stage in the public discourse only when demeaned and attacked because of its failure to prevent child abuse and a wide assortment of parent behaviours and child tragedies considered morally offensive. Sometimes, social work is held responsible for failures in the general area of thrusting people off welfare, for not pushing them into "the mainstream," for failing to get them to reform their behaviours and not "defraud" taxpayers who provide their sustenance.

Social work gets its lumps from the press and public because it has a record of immense inability to significantly diminish poverty and its associated social

11

problems, and because it is perceived as trying to mend poverty with variants of therapy. These, of course, are both futile endeavours, but they represent complex myths to which the public is seriously attached. And social workers often have seemed to lend themselves to the project of personality change as a way to leave poverty to enter the mainstream, meaning to conduct oneself acceptably and be employed. As we have seen, this idea has ancient origins.

It was awareness of the incongruity of therapy as a panacea for poverty that over time led social workers to embrace the idea of changing personalities through therapy. You could say that poverty was exchanged for personality as the venue for intervention. Personality was perceived as more alterable than poverty. Psyches were thought to be more malleable than a wage structure with built-in inequality that only the luckiest and most talented poor people could escape. Furthermore, psychoanalytic theory was interpreted to suggest that the underlying problem to failed lifestyles was to be found in the psyche.

Social structure and personality are an indivisible admixture of cause and effect. Nevertheless, social work has put its emphasis on personalities, feelings and lifestyles as primary targets of intervention. It could and did construct approaches combining theoretical attention to environment (renamed ecology, systems or social context). It could and did construct approaches addressed to bits and pieces of problems instead of shamelessly attacking "the total situation." Examples of these more modest approaches are brief treatment, crisis intervention, task-centered treatment, behaviour modification. However, no amount of rhetoric could de-emphasize the psyche.

Perennially engulfed in defining and redefining itself, social work's public posture is by turns reticent, clinging, aggressive, pompous, decent and virtuous. Its personnel appear in a variety of garbs from designer suits to the oldest torn blue jeans, its language ranging from ponderously academic to straight street jargon.

Barbara Wootton, in a classic 1959 essay on the nature of social work stated:

> [M]odern definitions of 'social casework,' if taken at their face value, involve claims to powers which verge upon omniscience and omnipotence: one can only suppose that those who perpetuate these claims in cold print must, for some as yet unexplained reason, have been totally deserted by their sense of humour (Wootton, 1959).

Nearly thirty years later, in 1987, the *Encyclopedia of Social Work* stated:

[T]he debate about the special niche and identity of the profession goes on....[T]he lack of a circumscribed and defined domain makes it difficult to interpret the profession to the larger public and to ward off competition from business administrators, psychologists, counselors, and various types of human resource experts and paraprofessionals for positions that social workers believe belong to them... (Khinduka, 1987: 691).

Social work is haunted by demands that it justify itself. Always on the search for explanations of its anomalous situation, social work has interpreted its problems as stemming from an assortment of unsolved problems. It has long thought it is misunderstood and needed better public relations; that its knowledge-base is insufficiently robust so that it must voraciously borrow from social science and psychiatry; that it is the victim of poor research methods which lack the ability to prove its effectiveness. The most current bitter appraisal of the ineffectiveness of the profession is by a pair of social work professors (Lindsey and Kirk, 1992) who call for a major overhaul of research education to position social work to acquire the authority it supposedly needs to take on the "problems that lie on social work's doorstep" — among them homelessness, welfare dependency, neglect and abuse of children, alcohol and substance abuse, crime and mental disorders" (p. 370).

This unhappy condition — weakness, invisibility, ambiguity — is at bottom a product of gender. It is only recently that the nature and effects of gender issues in social work are being recognized and studied. A great deal needs to be done to re-examine the history and reinterpret the past and its relationship to the present. The personnel in social work are overwhelmingly women. Over 400,000 persons in the labour force are called social workers. Seventy-three per cent are women, calculating out to nearly 300,000 women social work practitioners. More than 26 per cent are classified as mental health practitioners, but the nature of practice is that mental health is the dominant subject for intervention throughout all the practices (Hopps and Pinderhughes, 1987: 351–366). Of therapy practitioners who are women most of them are social workers, although it is increasingly common to disguise their professional discipline by adopting such non-identifying labels as "clinician."

Women acquired professional status in social work by creating new social institutions where they hoped to be respected and opening up opportunities for their own development and achievement (Muncy, 1991). They transformed depictions of female care-taking stereotypes into abstract ideas about treatment or therapy of individuals, families and groups. Social work virtually invented a panoply of abstractly described "methods" intended to name, describe and explain, to theorize ideas about care/protection/ treatment of socially "ill" persons. It is this triad of care/protection/treatment (CPT) which absolutely distinguishes the ideology of social work from all the other formal therapy professions. It is this CPT idea that underwrites social work's overriding claim of responsibility for and expertise in a whole shopping centre of social problems, often put forward as social work's mission. CPT provides social work with immense flexibility and justification for its claims over an expansive turf. Psychoanalysis was its lucky find, coming along and looking for a base just at the time when social work was in need of an interesting and upcoming body of thought to give it posh and portent. This marriage of convenience served both fields. Social workers became the silent partners of psychoanalysts (and their wives and lovers). That partnership, unequal and peculiar, fashioned modern therapeutics.

Social work's uniqueness among the therapy occupations is not properly understood. It is the most numerous therapy profession. It is strategically situated in public and private sector establishments so that it interacts with people of all classes, all living styles, most backgrounds and occupations. It is strong not because of its public image or its ability to display dominance, but because of its superior numbers and its expansive reach into every cranny in society. It is the disciplinary and the tutelary profession par excellence (Donzelot, 1979). Perceived as weak, it is stigmatized as women's work. It has cooperated, sometimes willingly but most often opportunistically, with the dominant male power structure to subordinate itself as a means of buying time, avoiding ambush and depreciation.

Understanding its overt powerlessness, social work sought and accepted male dominance of its occupational hierarchy and political economy. Its entrance as a recognized profession onto the national stage was orchestrated by Franklin Roosevelt's appointment of Harry Hopkins, a social worker, to head the Federal Emergency Relief Administration, the country's first modern public welfare program. This opened up positions at all levels for professionally educated women social workers. They accommodated themselves to paternal dominance. This was not a matter of a glass ceiling but rather a segmented workplace. As in the traditional family, women knew and kept their place if they wanted to get along. Leading women in the early part of this century were just beginning the struggle for independence and most were locked into an ideology that believed in the appropriateness of traditional women's roles.

CONCLUSION

The Therapeutic Idea is a concept that pervades the public mind, influences the shape of social policy and is perceived to be the means to produce personal well-being. It is an idea that is basic to the function of the therapy professions, among which social work plays a unique role, more important than is realized. The therapeutic idea, the practices that it spawns, its merging with governance, society and culture has created a pervasive hold on present society. The nature of this hold needs to be thoroughly investigated. The scientific basis of therapeutism is questionable. Its complex practices are difficult to analyze and evaluate. Most of all, there is a need to understand more about what these dominating ideas do in the lives of real people and to think more about what we want them to do — and not do.

ENDNOTES

1. Numbers of therapists and clients are exceedingly hard to come by. The system is far-flung, under many auspices, and there is no systematic or uniform method of data collection. These numbers have been put together for the American Psychological Association by Gary R. VandenBos, Nicholas A. Cummings, and Patrick H. Leon, 1992: 65–102. Also, *A Report of the Task Force on Social Work Research*, November 1991.
2. Philip Pinel (1745-1826). Appointed in 1793 director of Bicentre hospital and shortly thereafter of the Salpetriere. Major textbook published in 1809.

REFERENCES

Berger, P.L. (1977). Toward a sociological understanding of psychoanalysis. In *Facing up to modernity: Excursions in society, politics, and religion*, 23–34. New York: Basic Books.

Best, S. and D. Kellner. (1991). *Postmodern theory*. New York: Guilford Press.

Castel, R. (1988). *The regulation of madness*. Berkeley: University of California Press.

Dawley, A. (1991). *Struggles for justice: Social responsibility and the liberal state*. Cambridge: Harvard University Press.

Donzelot, J. (1979). *The policing of families*. New York: Pantheon Books.

Dreyfus, H.L. and P. Rabinow. (1982). *Beyond structuralism and hermeneutics*. Chicago: The University of Chicago Press.

Ehrenreich, J.H. (1985). *The altruistic imagination: A history of social work and social policy in the United States*. Ithaca: Cornell University Press.

Foucault, M. (1979). *Discipline and punish: The birth of the prison*, trans. A. Sheridan. New York: Vintage/Random House.

Freedheim, D.K. (ed.). (1992). *History of psychotherapy: A century of change.* Washington: American Psychological Association.

Grob, G.N. (1983). *Mental illness and American society, 1875-1940.* Princeton, New Jersey: Princeton University Press.

Grunbaum, A. (1984) *The foundations of psychoanalysis.* Berkeley: University of California Press.

Halmos, P. (1970). *The faith of the counsellors: A study in the theory and practice of social case work and psychotherapy.* New York: Schocken Books.

Hopps, J.G. and E.B. Pinderhughes. (1987). Profession of social work: Contemporary characteristics. In *Encyclopedia of social work, eighteenth edition*, 351–366. Silver Spring, Maryland: National Association of Social Workers.

Katz, M.B. (1986). *In the shadow of the poorhouse: A social history of welfare in America.* New York: Basic Books.

Klein, P. (1968). *From philanthropy to social welfare.* San Francisco: Jossey-Bass.

Khinduka, S.K. (1987). Social work and human services. In *Encyclopedia of social work, eighteenth edition, Volume Two*, 691. Silver Spring, Maryland: National Association of Social Workers.

Kuhn, T. (1970). *The structure of scientific revolutions.* Chicago: The University of Chicago Press.

Lindsey, D. and S.A. Kirk. (1992). The continuing crisis in social work research: Conundrum or solvable problem? An essay review. *Journal of Social Work Education* 28(3): 370–382.

London, P. (1964). *The modes and morals of psychotherapy.* New York: Holt, Rinehart and Winston.

Muncy, R. (1981). *Creating a female dominion in American reform: 1890-1935.* New York: Oxford University Press.

Pallone, N.J. (1992). Scientific and professional psychology. *Society* 30(1): 64–69.

Polsky, A.J. (1991). *The rise of the therapeutic state.* Princeton, New Jersey: Princeton University Press.

Report of the Task Force on Social Work Research. (November 1991). *Building social work knowledge for effective services and policies: A plan for research and development.* Austin, Texas.

Rieff, P. (1968). *The triumph of the therapeutic: Uses of faith after Freud.* New York: Harper and Row.

VandenBos, G.R., N.A. Cummings and P.H. DeLeon. (1992). A century of psychotherapy: Economic and environmental infulences. In *History of psychotherapy: A century of change,* ed. D.K. Freedhaim, 65–102. Washington: American Psychological Association.

Wilson, W.J. (ed.). (1989). The ghetto underclass: Social science perspectives. *Annals of the American Academy of Political and Social Science,* Special Issue, January: 501.

Wootton, B. (1959). *Social science and social pathology.* London: Allen and Unwin.

CHAPTER 2

FROM IMAGE TO SIMULACRA: THE MODERN/POSTMODERN DIVIDE AND SOCIAL WORK

ALLAN IRVING

Most of us have a sense, however vaguely felt, that our society, and for that matter the world, is undergoing intense irreversible transformations, radical change, as we increasingly inhabit a world of disorienting electronic flux and a supersaturated and surprisingly chaotic environment of information technology. It is evident that we have left modernity, best defined as a consumer society, behind and have entered a new era of postmodernism, defined as an electronic information society. Fredric Jameson argues in *Postmodernism: Or the Cultural Logic of Late Capitalism* (1991) that "full post-modernism" as defining the age emerges only when the modern becomes universal and therefore invisible. The splintered, fractured world of postmodernism that we inhabit, our cultural, social, political and economic context of the late twentieth century, is not a homogeneous entity or some sort of consciously directed movement; we are simply in it. It is elusive, nebulous, decentered and decentering; for cyberpunkers, those counterculture rebels of the 1990s, postmodernism is a dark brilliance, a bleak silent world "except for the glow of monitors and the crackle of telecommunications" (Bruner).

In *Postmodernism: The Twilight of the Real* (1990:1) Neville Wakefield observes that we live in a world of flux, a time "stripped of transcendent truths, linear arguments, solid foundations and neat resolutions" where structures don't last, grand theories ebb and fade, and "ambitions have half lives." Echoing

Wakefield it may be that, as social workers living in a postmodern world, our task is perhaps not so much to find ends or definitive solutions, but rather to live in, and try to make sense out of, a world where all promise and possibility of certainty has been withdrawn, perhaps forever (p. 151).

One of the favourite images of postmodern writers is that of pastiche, a collage or montage of colliding images. A not very good postmodern joke runs something like this: What flavour of ice-cream do postmodernists most enjoy? Pastichio of course. Jean Baudrillard describes in *The Ecstasy of Communication* (1987: 22) the 'ecstatic' celebration of the neutralization of meaning that a postmodern environment invariably engenders:

> We no longer partake of the drama of alienation, but are in the ecstasy of communication. And this ecstasy is obscene. Obscene is that which eliminates the gaze, the image and every representation. Obscenity is not confined to sexuality, because today there is a pornography of information and communication, a pornography of circuits and networks, of functions and objects in their legibility, availability, regulation and forced signification, capacity to perform, polyvalence, their free expression....

As we celebrate the technology of total communication we need to be aware of the ever-present danger of losing ourselves and our ties to others in cybernetic integration.

The postmodern era has been marked by a rhythm of uninhibited consumption where human consciousness actually now is produced in the act of consumption. It is a world where human relationships and our more traditional understandings of subjectivity seem on slippery, uncertain ground. This essay briefly examines some of the meanings of our postmodern world and how this defines our particular cultural, social and economic life of the late twentieth century. This will give some clues about what we as social workers are up against. To do this adequately it is necessary to first explore the notion of modernity as the stage through which we have now passed and which, as a period lasting from the Enlightenment of the eighteenth century and the rise of liberal/capitalist society, has profoundly shaped the development of the profession of social work.

The French social theorist, Jean-François Lyotard, defines postmodernism and hence modernism this way:

> the postmodern is based fundamentally upon the perception of the existence of a modern era that dates from the time of the Enlightenment and that now has run its course; and this modern

era was predicated on the notion of progress in knowledge, in the arts, in technology, and in human freedom as well, all of which was thought of as leading to a truly emancipated society: a society emancipated from poverty, despotism and ignorance. But all of us can see that development continues to take place without leading to the realization of any of these dreams of emancipation (quoted in Wakefield, p. 23).

It is important to bear in mind that discourses about both modernity and postmodernity have taken shape within a capitalist culture; in modernity, a capitalist ethic shaped by a Fordist-Keynesian paradigm of mass, standardized production and consumption, and in postmodernity, an ethic created out of much more flexible forms of capital accumulation, labour market organization and consumption patterns.

"The project of modernity," as the philosopher Jurgen Habermas calls it, stems largely from the vision of eighteenth-century Enlightenment philosophers of "objective science, universal morality and law, and autonomous art according to their inner logic;" in short, the establishment of a tradition of subject-centered reason. The governing metanarrative has been one of unending progress through technical rationality towards individual and social emancipation. Objective science, the power of universal reason and notions of progress and freedom would be turned to liberating human beings from their chains and many of the irrationalities that had characterized the pre-modern age. Enlightenment philosophers like Condorcet were possessed of "the extravagant expectation that the arts and sciences would promote not only the control of natural forces but also understanding of the world and of the self, moral progress, the justice of institutions and even the happiness of human beings." In the writings of the eighteenth-century philosophers (Montesquieu, Rousseau, Condorcet, Hume) the essential ingredients of modern thought regarding the value of science, the power of reason, inexorable, unending progress, come vividly to life. In creating the intellectual and moral foundations for modernity the Enlightenment thinkers paved the way for an approach which argued that natural and social reality would be revealed through the practice of proper scientific methods of inquiry. The power of science to create unlimited progress grew until it came to have a stranglehold on our imaginations. We became convinced that more advanced forms of life could be created through various social technologies, hence the rise of the modern social sciences and the deep and abiding belief that social life could be reorganized and that social problems reduced, if not entirely eliminated, through the rational and rigorous application of scientific technique and the structured use of technology (Habermas, 1981:9, 1987:74; Harvey, 12-13).

21

The central thrust of modernity has been to invent order, promote certainty and, most important, perhaps to link technology and progress. A large part of the modern task, and one in which social work has played no small role, has been to get control over both nature and social life and to refashion a social world in line with blueprints forged in the ideological context of liberal notions of progress and derived from the imperatives of science, reason and technology. Philosopher Charles Taylor, in *The Malaise of Modernity* (chapter 1) , has laid out three aspects of our experience of the modern world. The first is the growth of individualism, where we no longer view ourselves as part of some larger order that defines us, a cosmic order, a "great chain of being." Individualism coupled with liberal capitalism has gradually eroded the bonds of community and any sense of higher purpose in what has been called the 'disenchantment' of the world.

Second, Taylor describes the primacy of instrumental reason, which involves the most efficient or economical application of means to any given end: we are all only too familiar with terms like "maximum efficiency" and "cost-benefit analysis." Instrumental reason means that things that ought to be determined by other criteria will be decided in terms of efficiency and other imperatives of this kind. Rather than independent ends, what the social and moral good ought to be, our lives and actions will be taken over and obliterated by demands to maximize output, by the demands of economic growth which are used constantly to justify the unequal distribution of wealth and income and contribute to our insensitivity to the environment, as graphically set out in Bill McKibben's *The End of Nature* (1989). The primacy of instrumental reason is reflected in the huge importance we assign to technology. Technophilia, the infatuation with technological innovation, is part of what lies behind the wish for a technical fix for problems which lie ultimately in the political, economic, cultural and moral realm. It is not, however, just enchantment or infatuation that explains the vice-like grip that we are held in by our technological surround. As cultural historian David Noble has observed, "it is the preservation or enhancement of an existing system of domination that is both served and masked by infantile dreams of technological salvation" (quoted in Smart: 63). Max Horkheimer and Theodore Adorno, in *The Dialectic of Enlightenment* (1972), persuasively argued that instrumental reason, carried to its logical conclusion, leads not just to the domination and oppression of nature but to the domination of human beings and to "a nightmare condition of self-domination," so evident in a society where the commodification of all aspects of existence has emerged. For Max Weber, instrumental reason had led, by the early twentieth century, to "the iron cage" of bureaucracy (Harvey: 13).

Third, Taylor argues, a society forged from individualism and instrumental reason entails a certain loss of freedom; we have for example designed cities around the private automobile rather than well-developed public transportation, making a life-style free of dependence on the car a difficult alternative to maintain.

Social workers are acutely aware of how often they are undervalued in a system where they want to provide humane sensitive caring as opposed to specialists with high-tech knowledge. We are all too aware, as Taylor, points out, of how technology and its overwhelmingly dominant place in our lives has led to a loss of resonance, depth and richness in our human interactions with one another. Liberal-techno society results in people "enclosed in their own hearts," where the vague dissatisfactions of private life outweigh those of public interaction and public discourse. Moral ends are eclipsed constantly in the face of rampant instrumental reason. Marshall Berman, in his wonderful book *All That is Solid Melts into Air: the Experience of Modernity* (1982: 13, 15), points to the horrors, ambiguities and ironies of modern life. To be modern means to live in an environment, says Berman, that "promises us adventure, power, joy, transformation of ourselves and the world, and at the same time that threatens to destroy everything we have, everything we know." Modernity, he suggests, "pours us all into a maelstrom of perpetual disintegration and renewal, of struggle and contradiction, of ambiguity and anguish." To be modern, as Marx said, was to be part of a universe in which "all that is solid melts into air."

The modernism that emerged in the early decades of the twentieth century was characterized by new conditions of production — the machine, the factory, urbanization — new systems of transport and communication and a whole new approach to consumption — the rise of mass markets, advertising and mass fashion. There was a fascination with speed and power and the machine — houses and cities were conceived as "machines for living in." The car, which has more than any other artifact defined and shaped twentieth century culture, is of course just that: a machine for living in. It hermetically seals us off from one another as we aimlessly hurtle back and forth. One of the key works of early twentieth century modernism was F.W. Taylor's *The Principles of Scientific Management* (1911), which set out how work and the worker could be organized along scientific lines to be more efficient and more productive. Hence the language of Taylorism entered the language of social analysis. Three years later in 1914, Henry Ford set in motion the first example of assembly line production in Dearborn, Michigan; thus establishing the culture of mass consumption as the organizing principle of twentieth century life. The term Fordism is in many respects synonymous with modernism.

The twentieth century has been one long, growing, calling into question the project of modernity. Two important late nineteenth and early twentieth century critics were the sociologist Max Weber and the existential philosopher Friedrich Nietzsche. Weber recognized that the boundless optimism of the Enlightenment thinkers was a bitter and ironic illusion. The link they forged between science/rationality and universal human freedom would turn out to be misleading and ultimately false. The real legacy of the Enlightenment, when properly understood, was a victory for purposive-instrumental rationality, a form of rationality which proved to be insidious, infecting the entire range of social and cultural life including economic structures, law, bureaucratic administration and even the arts. The growth of instrumental rationality led instead away from the concrete realization of universal freedom to what Weber characterized as the "iron cage" of bureaucratic rationality from which there is no escape. Who does not experience almost daily the claustrophobia and dehumanization of this iron cage of bureaucracy? (Harvey: 15).

Nietzsche called attention to the terrifying idea that lurking just below the surface of modern life bucked and plunged wild forces of disorder, destruction, alienation and despair. All there really was, he claimed, was an ocean of creative destruction and destructive creation. The twentieth century soon provided evidence enough of just what Nietzsche meant. Two violently destructive world wars, death camps and the holocaust, the threat of nuclear annihilation, ecological disaster and so much suffering in so many other ways.

In *The Dialectic of Enlightenment* (1972) the critical theorists Max Horkheimer and Theodore Adorno advanced the startling thesis that the Enlightenment project, the project of modernity, would turn on itself, and instead of a positive quest for human emancipation we would end up with a system of universal oppression in the name of human liberation. The unsettling novels of Kafka and the negative utopias of Huxley, Orwell, Zamyatin and Margaret Atwood's *The Handmaid's Tale* all speak to this dreadful possibility. The central argument of Horkheimer and Adorno is that the real logic behind Enlightenment rationality was a logic of domination and oppression.

Denunciations of technology as dehumanization and as the creator of human alienation have become part of the modernist critique. One of the interesting things that has happened is that in the condition of postmodernity, which since the late 1960s has come more and more to characterize our existence, technology has been recast as information technology in the mould no longer now of alienation but of deliverance. Theodore Roszak, one of the most influential critics of modernity and technology over the past twenty-five years, argues that we have been reduced to helpless awe and dependence before "the arsenal of wonders," as he calls the society created by science and technology and the consequent urban-industrial uniformity. We are seldom able to imagine alternatives, and constantly defer to scientific-technical-professional expertise which, if allowed to continue, will lead, as Rozak so powerfully argued in *Where the Wasteland Ends: Politics and Transcendence in Postindustrial Society* (1972: 64-65),

> to an air-conditioned nightmare of endemic malfunction and slapdash improvisation. Glowing advertisements of undimished progress will continue to rain down on us from official quarters; there will always be well-researched predictions of light at the end of every tunnel. There will be dazzling forecasts of limitless affluence. There will even be much real affluence. But nothing will ever quite work the way the salesman promised; the abundance will be mired in organizational confusion and bureaucratic malaise, constant environmental emergency... breakdowns in communication, overburdened social services.... The scene will be indefinably sad and shoddy despite the veneer of orthodox optimism.... Everything will take on that vile tackiness which only plastic can assume, the look of things decaying that were never suppose to grow old....

The person in Canada who best articulated the attack on the link between technology and progress was the philosopher George Grant. Although he died in 1988 many still look to Grant for an illumination of the darkness of technological society. As William Christian observed in his recent biography, Grant's writings are shot through with doubts about the idea of progress which to our unenlightened minds always presents itself as inevitable; and about the idea of technological mastery which is represented by modern thinkers as a neutral means to a justified end. For Grant, the relentless quest for technological mastery came to mean the opposite of what the ancients, Plato and Augustine, had called the Good. Modernity for Grant was not motion leading to rest but more action leading endlessly on. It was Grant's contention that modernity made contemplation, reverence and awe impossible. Initially Grant accepted that it might be possible to control technology in the name of a morality that had independent standing; later, however, he abandoned that position. Technology he felt had become so all pervasive that it now was impossible to have any outside standpoint from which to judge its effects. The religion of mastery, as he called it, was a faith so powerful that no one could effectively challenge it. A powerful theme running through all Grant's work is that there are forces loose in the world that are leading remorselessly to deterioration and decline.

Growing ever more pervasive in contemporary life is a broad social\cultural formation known as postmodernity. David Harvey, in *The Condition of Postmodernity* (1989), explains the transition from modernity to postmodernity as largely related to the changing nature of capitalism, from a Fordist-Keynesian set of arrangements to one of increasingly flexible accumulation and corresponding changes in patterns of production and consumption that occurred from about 1973 onwards. The countercultural and antimodernist movements of the 1960s prepared the way for the emergence of postmodernism.

Capitalist accumulation and the attendant process of commodification has developed to the point where it is without bounds; it now extends into all aspects of individual and collective life. For Frederic Jameson, as the title of his wide-ranging book *Postmodernism, or The Cultural Logic of Late Capitalism* (1991) indicates, postmodernism is nothing more than the cultural logic of late capitalism. Postmodernity seriously calls into question the driving force of modernity to get absolute control over nature and social organization, "to redesign or refashion the world in accordance with a blueprint derived from reason." The whole project of modernity has been devoted to creating order, manufacturing certainty and fashioning linear progress. Through the lens of postmodernity it is possible to see that the modernist quest for order, certainty and unending progress also created ambivalence, contingency, dissatisfaction and restlessness. Zygmunt Bauman has observed that postmodernity shows us the limits and limitations of modernity. Postmodernity, he suggests, means facing up to the fact that "certainty is not to be," that "the growth of knowledge expands the field of ignorance," and that "our journey has no clear destination" (Smart: 213, 218, 219; Bauman: 244; Wakefield: 20; Harvey: 50-1).

If we accept the notion that our form of late-twentieth-century life is defined largely by the cultural surround of postmodernism, then, according to Jurgen Habermas, this means "the end of the Enlightenment" and a form of life "beyond the horizon of the tradition of reason in which European modernity once understood itself." As a cultural form and style postmodernism revolves around diversity, "displays a penchant for pastiche, and adopts an 'inclusivist' philosophy, advocating eclectic use of elements from the past" (Habermas, 1987: 4; Smart: 168,185). The French high priest of postmodernism, Jean Baudrillard describes the postmodern as

> the characteristic of a universe where there are no more definitions possible. It is a game of definitions which matters. It is also the possibility of resuscitating images at the second level, ironically of course. It all revolves around an impossible definition. One is

> no longer in a history of art or a history of forms. They have been
> deconstructed, destroyed. In reality, there is no more reference
> to forms. It has all been done. The extreme limit of these
> possibilities has been reached. It has destroyed itself. It has
> deconstructed its entire universe. So all that are left are pieces.
> All that remains to be done is to play with the pieces. Playing
> with the pieces — that is postmodern (quoted in Kellner: 116).

Literary critic Terry Eagleton, writing in the *Times Literary Supplement* in 1987, suggested that postmodernism's stance towards cultural tradition involves a kind of "contrived depthlessness" which "undermines all metaphysical solemnities." Postmodernism sounds the death knell for all metanarratives "whose secretly terroristic function was to ground and legitimate the illusion of a 'universal' human history." Science, philosophy, religion now must accept that they are just another set of narratives and give up all claims to universal metaphysical status. Postmodernist thought favours ("privileges") heterogeneity and difference, fragmentation and indeterminacy, and holds all universal or "totalizing" discourses in utter contempt. Postmodernism no longer accepts the positivist belief that human knowledge is simply an empirical mirroring and instead argues that knowledge is an invention of the mind by which we all endeavour to align our experience with our needs and values. In short, reality is made not found (Harvey: 7-8; Sass: 96).

In *The Postmodern Condition: A Report on Knowledge* (1984), Jean Francois Lyotard offers up a penetrating critique of modernist metanarratives and, in fact, defines postmodernism as "incredulity towards metanarratives." Modernism has largely legitimated itself through its appeals to "grand narratives." Modernism sought to ground itself in history and accepted that there is some kind of working out of an overall Enlightenment purpose. With little hesitation, postmodernism sweeps aside modernist foundationalism and teleology. Lyotard also argues that modernism is hopelessly tied to a belief, largely anachronistic, that there is always the possibility of an overall unity through which contradictions can be resolved. He contends that, in view of post-industrial developments in computerization and information science, "the old principle that the acquisition of knowledge is indissociable from the training of minds, or even of individuals, is becoming obsolete and will become even more so.... Knowledge is and will be produced in order to be sold, it is and will be consumed in order to be valorized in a new production: in both cases, the goal is exchange. Knowledge ceases to be an end in itself, it loses its 'use-value.'" Like many postmodernist thinkers, Lyotard is intrigued by all the new possibilities for information and knowledge production and analysis. For Lyotard, the advent of postmodern culture is the result of major changes in the language of communication in late capitalist society (Lyotard: xxiii, xxiv, 4 14; Harvey: 49; Crook: 151).

While there are many antihumanist strains in Lyotard's conception of the organization of postmodernist knowledge which are cause for concern, there are many positive aspects as well. With its rejection of grand governing metanarratives, postmodernism opens up the possibility of beginning to hear other voices — those of women, gays, blacks and other visible minorities, colonized peoples, the working class, religious groups — that were forced into silence for so long. One of the most attractive aspects of postmodernist thought is its deep concern with "otherness." A number of postmodernists, in fact, have taken modernity to task for its insensitivity and intellectual imperialism in claiming to speak for others in totalizing and universalizing discourses. A good example is Carol Gilligan's feminist work, *In a Different Voice: Psychological Theory and Women's Development* (1982), which censures the male bias which traditionally has been used to describe the stages in the moral development of personality. Another is Elizabeth Wilson's *The Sphinx in the City: Urban Life, the Control of Disorder, and Women* (1991), in which she examines the contrasts and possibilities of cities from the perspective of the "others" of postmodern life: racial minorities, sexual groups and disempowered classes. Her central thesis is that the city offers women, in particular, freedom from patriarchal and family authority, and that there is a need to confront and challenge male notions of order in urban planning. Postmodernism embraces fragmentation, ephemerality and the eddies and swirls of chaotic change. Foucault encouraged us to "develop action, thought and desires by proliferation, juxtaposition and disjunction," and "to prefer what is positive and multiple, difference over uniformity, flows over unities, mobile arrangements over systems" (Harvey: 42, 44, 47, 48). It is apparent that postmodernism is a term that covers a wide range of objects, texts, practices, experiences and conditions; as Dick Hebdidge observes, everything from the "decor of a room, the design of a building...the construction of a record...an anti-technological tendency within epistemology...the collective chagrin and morbid projections of a post-war generation of baby boomers confronting disillusioned middle age...a new phase in commodity fetishism, the 'decentring' of the subject, an 'incredulity towards metanarratives,' a sense...of 'placelessness.'..or a generalized substitution of spatial for temporal conditions" (Hebdidge: 182; Smart: 199).

There is a much bleaker, nihilistic side to postmodernism as well, depicted, for example, in Ridley Scott's early 1980s film *Blade Runner*. Based on a science fiction novel by Philip K. Dick, the film takes place in a decaying urban-scape, Los Angeles, in the year 2019, and graphically portrays a city and world winding

28

down. Evocative in its dark mood of the film noir genre of the late 1940s, *Blade Runner* captures perfectly Baudrillard's horrifying prediction of a world moving from a preoccupation with image to a total simulacrum (the image without an original). In our real world of urban blight and decay, unemployment and the countless homeless wandering the streets of late-twentieth-century cities draw attention to the fact that, indeed, all is far from well in a postmodern metropolis.

Great shifts in the organization of the labour market run like a strong current underneath the pattern of contemporary life. It has been estimated that, by the end of the decade, less than half the workforce in the industrialized world will be employed full time. Part-timers, temporary workers, and the unemployed make up more and more of the labour force in postmodern capitalist society. The implications are profound: far less security and stability and increasing anxiety and uncertainty for individuals and families caught irretrievably in the vast alterations set loose by flexible forms of capital accumulation. The political economy of postmodern society favours a neo-conservative agenda of free-market forces and privatization and a downgrading of the welfare state. The private is elevated over the public; people plan more for themselves than for their communities. One of the great civilizing forces of the twentieth century has been an increasing role for the state, for the public realm; with the transition to postmodernism this civilizing influence of the public is in danger of being obliterated, of imploding into private cyberspace.

The realization that the modern project is on the rocks can lead to despair or it can open the door for conceptions of alternative social futures: new social movements, new forms of resistance in feminist and aboriginal struggles, ecology movements, urban/rural protest movements and other marginalized constituencies. Responding to the postmodernist crisis can mean, in the words of Dick Hebdidge, "the opening up to critical discourse of lines of enquiry which were formerly prohibited...the opening up of institutional and discursive spaces within which more fluid and plural social and sexual identities may develop...the erosion of triangular formations of power and knowledge with the expert at the apex and the 'masses' at the base, if in a word, it enhances our collective and democratic sense of possibility." In the postmodernist surround the false imperatives of science and technology crumble and give way to new forms of analysis and understanding and new forms of social action. As Foucault has remarked, "things can be changed, fragile as they are, held together more by complex but transitory historical contingency than by anthropological constraints" (Hebdidge: 226; Foucault quoted in Smart: 221).

E.J. Urwick, a social philosopher who was head of the department of social work from 1927-37 (then called the department of social science) at the University of Toronto argued in many writings that there could not be a science of social life; that social workers had to be aware of the fatal limitations of the scientific method; that being content with mere facts would close our eyes to the ends, to visions of the good, to values, ideals and utopian reconstruction even if this were to occur only in the imagination. Social workers, Urwick stated in a 1940 essay, whose aim is, in essence, the building of a new Jerusalem, must let their minds dwell on the idea of the good rather than concentrate on mechanical techniques and methods (Irving: liv, lxi).

As social workers, social scientists and social philosophers we need to reject the view that all we need to do is to apply, guided by the scientific imperative, the value-free techniques of description and measurement to social and individual problems. In many respects to measure is to destroy. In her recent and wonderfully evocative novel, *The Fourth Archangel* (p. 294) Saskatchewan author Sharon Butala, has one of her main characters, Amy Sparrow say at the end of the novel: "It is the idea of progress that has killed us. We were whole the way we were, but we dreamt of progress and our dreams destroyed us. It has always been this way." As social workers and social actors we always have to come back to the question of human will and values, where philosophy, literature and history, not technology and science, are our surest guides into an uncertain, terrifying and even tragic future.

The great difficulty we are up against is that in many respects postmodernism is simply an extension of the darkness of modernity, but without the traditional humanist certainties and the universal truths that anchored modernity. Habermas argues strenuously that the project of modernity can still offer a way out — that the Enlightenment project of universal reason is still our best bet. The question we have to ask is: Is it too late? Have we, as Baudrillard would have us believe, entered the realm of the hyperreal — the society of total simulation? "Modernity," wrote Baudelaire in 1863, "is the transient, the fleeting, the contingent; it is one half of art, the other being the eternal and the immutable" (quoted in Harvey: 12). In the postmodern darkness the search for the eternal seems often impossible and yet, at the end of his last great book *Words with Power* (p. 313), Northrop Frye writes,

> When we become intolerably oppressed by the mystery of human existence and by what seems the utter impotence of God to do or even care anything about human suffering, we enter the stage of Eliot's "word in the desert," and hear all the rhetoric of ideologues, expurgating, revising, setting straight, rationalizing, proclaiming the time of renovation. After that, perhaps the terrifying and welcome voice may begin, annihilating everything we thought we knew, and restoring everything we have never lost.

30

REFERENCES

Baudrillard, J. (1987). *The ecstasy of communication.* New York: Semiotext.

Berman, M. (1982). *All that is solid melts into air: The experience of modernity.* New York: Simon and Schuster.

Bruner, L. (1993) "Cyberpunk." *Toronto Star,* 28 February 1993.

Butala, S. (1992). *The fourth archangel.* Toronto: Harper Collins Publisher Ltd.

Christian, W. (1993). *George Grant: A biography.* Toronto: University of Toronto Press.

Crook, S. (1991). *Modernist radicalism and its aftermath.* London: Routledge.

Frye, N. (1990). *Words with power.* New York: Viking.

Habermas, J. (1981). Modernity versus postmodernity. *New German Critique* no. 22.

Habermas, J. (1987). *The philosophical discourse of modernity.* Cambridge: Polity Press.

Harvey, D. (1989). *The condition of postmodernity.* Cambridge: Basil Blackwell, Inc.

Hebdidge, D. (1988). *Hiding in the light: On images and things.* London: Routledge.

Horkheimer, M. and T. Adorno. (1973). *Dialectic of enlightenment.* London: Allen Lane.

Irving, J. A. (1948). The social philosophy of E.J. Urwick. In *The values of life,* ed. E.J. Urwick. Toronto: University of Toronto Press.

Jameson, F. (1991). *Postmodernism or the cultural logic of late capitalism.* Durham: Duke University Press.

Kellner, D. (1989). *Jean Baudrillard: From Marxism to postmodernism and beyond.* Stanford: Standford University Press.

Lyotard, J-F. (1991). *The postmodern condition: A report on knowledge.* Minneapolis: University of Minnesota Press.

Pangle, T. (1992). *The enobling of democracy: The challenge of the postmodern era.* Baltimore: The Johns Hopkins University Press.

Sass, L. A. (1994). The epic of disbelief: The postmodernist turn in psychoanalysis. *Partisan Review*. Winter:96-110.

Smart, B. (1992). *Modern conditions, postmodern controversies*. New York: Routledge, Chapman & Hall.

Taylor, C. (1991). *The malaise of modernity*. Concord, Ontario: House of Anansi.

Wakefield, N. (1990). *Postmodernism: The twilight of the real*. Winchester, Massachussetts: Pluto.

Chapter 3

Feminist Postmodernism and the Challenge of Diversity

Catrina Brown

Women's voices are often absent in the teaching and practice of social work despite the fact that most social workers and their clients are women.[1] Mainstream social work upholds and reinforces the structural social oppression of women as a group as women's experiences continue to be pathologized and removed from the context of their lives. At best the traditional practice of social work functions to manage women's problems; at worst it revictimizes and deepens women's oppression. We cannot change social work from an institution of social control to one which fosters social change unless we begin to include women's voices in social work education and confront the very structure of knowledge itself. Contemporary debates within feminist postmodernism have directly addressed the ideological and gendered construction of knowledge, and are, therefore, helpful to the challenges of diversity and inclusion in social work theory and practice.

Social workers are trained to fit into bureaucractic social welfare institutions with traditional policies and clinical interventions. It is rare for social work education to make understanding social oppression and the need for social change central. In particular, the power relations and structures which oppress women are not adequately acknowledged in conventional social work theory. Social problems are defined through systems and ecological theories which fail to address the asymmetrical power relations of society. Further, the knowledge provided by these organizations and theories is presented as objective, a stance which is both integral to conventional theory and which obscures its institutional privilege. The competing world views of marginalized and less powerful social groups are not reflected in theory or in institutional practices.

The hegemonic or dominant ideology central to mainstream social work assumes that objective truth exists and can be discovered by "value-free" social inquiry. Yet, one is always a perspectival knower; one always knows from a particular location, which is only masked when knowledge production does not identify the location of the knower through an assumption of neutral objectivity. The diversity of people's experiences are obscured and homogenized through these "objectified" accounts. Such truth claims invariably represent the interests of the social elite, inasmuch as they present the social and political *status quo* as "objective reality," thereby misrepresenting and excluding those without social power. Theories predicated on a privileged but unacknowledged class and androcentric standpoint ignore and distort the experiences of women, resulting in social work practice based on oppressive theories, which in turn oppress women.

Feminist social workers need to begin deconstructing the truth claims made by traditional social work. We need to question what version of reality is being produced. We need to question who is defining the reality that is presented as objectified knowledge. Who is the knower, and what is their social location? Some of the insights of femininst postmodernism can contribute to the building of a new knowledge base in social work.

Postmodernism as an epistemogical shift can challenge social work theory, practice and pedagogy to examine the hegemonic and exclusionary world view that tends to dominate the field, and thus encourage a more inclusive and representative practice of social work. Social work may then learn to become more clearly cognizant of a world organized around categories such as gender, race, class and sexual orientation. Postmodernism seeks to discover a way of recognizing the "other" and the multiplicity of identities by attending to the problems of difference and exclusion, which prevail in both liberal and radical thought and practice.

The fragmentary and transitory character of experience and identity has been emphasized in postmodernist thought. Yet, "identity politics" are central to the postmodern theoretical and political enterprise. The fluidity of postmodernism, its efforts to abandon fixed categories and its rejection of enlightenment conceptions of a single knowable reality, makes problematic the concept of a fixed identity. Whether one is a woman, black or lesbian often defines *a priori* the "political correctness" of the knower.

Postmodernism can be described as ambivalent to the culture of identity politics. On the one hand its attention to difference has contributed to the development of a politics based upon identity. On the other hand postmodern anti-essentialism rejects identity politics and the hierarchy of oppression, which have become the dominant response to the theoretical and political issues of difference.

Postmodernism can offer social work insights into the limitations of identity politics, particularly as social work begins to stress anti-sexist and anti-racist practice. Social work can also benefit from postmodernism's critique of the "authority of experience," which dominates feminist theory, practice and pedagogy. The postmodern view that the "authority of experience" produces an exclusionary, essentialist and ultimately de-politicized understanding of the social world can perhaps provide direction to social workers concerned about how to approach the crucial question of diversity. Despite these contributions I nonetheless suggest that the postmodern project of deconstruction, or of exposing the conservative bias in the liberal humanist tradition of modernism, falls short of its promise to offer alternative conceptions of the social world and, with these, concrete mechanisms for social change.

Postmodernism has shaken the foundation of knowledge, challenging the traditions of western political thought arising in the modern era. The traditional ways we have learned to understand subjectivity, reason and science, truth and epistemology have all been exposed as fundamentally flawed (Flax, 1990). Postmodernism has been involved in a project of deconstructing, pulling apart and destabilizing the hegemonic or dominant ideological framework and biases within modernist thought.

There is no one view of postmodernism within postmodern feminism, indeed there is not even agreement on a definition. It is clear, however, that postmodernism is a reaction to or a departure from modernism and its premises. The postmodern influence on feminism has resulted in a rethinking of the concepts central to feminism. Postmodern feminism addresses issues of inclusion, exclusion, diversity, essentialism and the foundation of what has been called knowledge itself. Feminist postmodernism, therefore, raises central issues for feminist knowledge and for understanding a gendered social world.

Feminism's recognition that the universalizing and essentializing of women's experiences is problematic has led to a convergence between feminism and postmodernism. The apparent unity of the women's movement has been exposed as a construction of exclusions and differences. Postmodern feminism, therefore, reflects the need for feminism to come to terms with the plurality of women's experiences. The growth of postmodern feminist theory is at least, in part, a response to the political crisis of mainstream feminism when confronted with this pluralism.

Two issues in particular concern feminist postmodernism. First, its critique of modernist epistemology exposes the way traditional definitions of truth in western political thought have both excluded and falsely universalized women. Second, feminist postmodernism addresses the issue of difference by stressing the need to recognize plurality or the heterogeneity of women's experiences. Women's experiences must not be totalized — race, class, ethnicity and sexual orientation for example must be specified.

Feminist postmodernism claims to reveal how the social relations of power are obscured, and alternative or competing frames are rendered invisible within traditional thought. It critiques the bias, politics and power concealed within objectified knowledge. Theoretically, feminist postmodernism allows for a connection to be made between knowledge, social reality and social power.

There is no one "Truth" according to postmodern feminism; there are instead, many standpoints, many ways of knowing. However, the rejection of positivist epistemology is not new for feminism or the left. Feminism has been strongly influenced by the critical thinking and the objectives of social change that Marxist and critical theory have brought to bear on our understanding of science as a social construct inseparable from the institutions of ruling and power in society. What is different within feminist postmodernism is its new emphasis on inclusion, diversity and representation. These issues of diversity now dominate feminist discourse and practice. Postmodern feminist theory has begun to redress feminism's history of unconscious racism and elitism (Bordo, 1990, p. 135). Women of colour, lesbian women, disabled women and poor women are challenging white-middle-class feminist perspectives, which have presumed to speak for unified women. So while feminism has long been critical of the androcentrism of theory and practice, feminist critique has now turned on itself.

Postmodern feminism recognizes and emphasizes the multiplicity of women's identities. This has led to criticism from some feminist theorists who suggest that the current focus on multiplicity and difference may render feminist politics impotent. The fragmentation of the women's movement into diverse groups reflects an emphasis on the differences rather than the similarities between women's experiences. Some feel this fragmentation and conflict within the women's movement may demobilize the possibility of effective social action and change.

Because feminism today places its focus on women's differences and diversities, the question of whether we can even talk about women as a category has arisen. Social categories such as "women" are fragmented by race, class and historical particularity (Bordo, 1990, p. 133). Denise Riley has raised considerable debate about the extent to which we can continue to use the category of women (1988). The focus on the diversity of women's social locations has challenged the idea that there is a unified or homogenous category of women. This challenge is the logical extension of the initial critique of modernist feminism, which often treated the categories of men and women as fixed, immutable or essential. Frequently, feminist theory has employed an already fully constituted and essentialist category of "woman." This suggests an uncritical and unself-conscious acceptance of a patriarchal category. Diana Fuss defines essentialism in her book, *Essentially Speaking. Feminism, Nature, and Difference:*

> Essentialism is most commonly understood as a belief in the real, true essence of things, the invariable and fixed properties which define the "whatness" of a given entity. In feminist theory, the idea that men and women, for example, are identified as such on the basis of transhistorical, eternal, immutable essences has been unequivocally rejected by many anti-essentialist poststructuralist feminists concerned with resisting any attempts to naturalize human nature (1989, p. xi).

Although we know that the category of women has problems, can we abandon it as some postmodern theorists would have us do? Postmodern theorists may have deconstructed gender in such a way as to depoliticize women's experiences in patriarchal society. For instance, some talk about "postgendered" or "dissipated identities." We need to avoid using the category of women as though it were natural, ahistorical, essential or unified. But as both Denise Riley (1988) and Judith Butler (1992) argue, we also need to preserve the tension between accepting, valuing and rejecting the category of women as it now exists.

Riley's interrogation of the category of women in *"Am I That Name?" Feminism and the Category of 'Women' in History,* has been contested by those who believe it undermines feminism (1988). In response to such critiques, Riley argues we can both question the cohesive identity of women and maintain a feminist politic. Identity is double-edged according to Riley who points to the dilemma of essentialism: "women can suffer from too much identification" (1992, p. 122). Butler also challenges the assumption that politics requires a stable subject (1992, p. 4). There is, she believes, an authoritarian element hidden in this position, one which implies there can be no political opposition to this claim. Butler instead critiques the foundational premises of categories, and by examining what authorizes categories such as the "subject" or "women" she attempts to "relieve it of its foundational weight," not discard it (1992, p. 8).

Like the category of women, difference itself needs to be problematized rather than treated as fact. The concept of difference is embedded within social relations and, therefore, like social relations must be subject to interrogation. Christina Crosby questions the ideology of difference in theory:

> It is impossible to ask how "differences" is constituted as a concept, so "differences" become substantive, something in themselves — race, class, gender — as though we knew already what this incommensurate triumvirate means! (1992, p. 137) ....
> That is, knowlege, if it is to avoid the circularity of ideology, must read the process of differentiation, not look for differences (p. 140).

Thus there is now the difficulty of trying to combine a non-essentialized, non-universalized understanding of women's lives with social change and political struggle. Adopting an essentialized category of women may further entrench women within patriarchal social relations. Feminist consciousness and feminist activism continue to struggle with the "tension between the preservation of gender consciousness and identity (as a source of political unity and alternative vision) and the deconstruction of 'gender prescriptions' which limit human choice and possibility" (Bordo, 1990, p. 153).

Yet, we need to avoid the simple polarization of essentialism and constructionism, the idea that "differences are constructed, not innate" (Fuss, 1989, p. xii). In an effort to avoid the "essentialism of essentialism," and the impasse in feminist theory between essentialist and anti-essentialist positions, Fuss's strategy of exploring how essentialism is deployed in the feminist therapy discourse is helpful (p. xii).

The slogan " the personal is political" has been foundational or axiomatic to most feminist theory, pedagogy and practice. All paradigms of feminist thought have tended to adopt standpoint theory's dependence on the "authority of experience" in the production of knowledge, truth and social change (Fuss 1989; Haug, 1992, p. 8). The "personal is political" and standpoint theory emphasize the inherent "truth" in women's experience. Epistemologically, standpoint theory attempts to provide a theory of knowledge from the position of women. It is based on the assumption that because women are outside the ruling class they are better able to provide an account of reality that exposes the way the world is actually structured. The "authority of experience" is then central to the production of knowledge about women. Beginning with the standpoint of women is justified as a response to the invisibility of women in androcentric and objectified accounts of the social world (McLure, 1992).

While feminism has made women's experience central, postmodernism has rejected this emphasis suggesting that it is a part of the creation of a universalized, essentialized, uniform and immutable notion of "the woman" as a category. Feminists, however, are reluctant to accept this criticism, as the female experience has become virtually sacrosanct in response to the dominance of androcentrism and the invisibility of women in most theory. According to Fuss, "theories of feminist pedagogy, the category of natural female experience is often held against (and posited as a corrective to) the category of imposed masculinist ideology" (1989, p. 114).

Fuss, raises important questions about the "authority of experience." She asks "[e]xactly what counts as 'experience,' and should we defer to it in pedagogical situations? Does experience of oppression confer special jurisidiction over the right to speak about that oppression? Can we only speak, ultimately, from the so-called 'truth' of our experiences, or are all empirical ways of knowing analytically suspect?" (1989, p. 113).

Dorothy Smith (1987; 1990) and Frigga Haug (1992) also question the focus on women's experience in feminist theory and practice. They suggest that we need to be concerned with how these experiences are socially organized. Fuss, Haug, and Smith, all recognize that experience itself is "ideologically cast" (Fuss 1989, p. 114) and socially constructed. Haug reminds us that individuals cannot give objective accounts of themselves, rather they subjectively construct and transform them (1992, p. 9). She states, "individuals turn and twist, change and falsify, repress and forget events, pursuing, what is in fact no more than an ideological construction of individuality, giving oneself an identity of the present to which the 'facts' of the past are subordinated.... Human beings transform the conditions of their lives until their existence becomes relatively uncontradictory" (p. 9). Haug, like Smith, focuses on the process by which women's experiences are put together, rather than simply taking them on face value.

Joan Scott has similarly problematized experience and concludes that it cannot be eliminated as a category within feminist politics:

> Experience is at once always an interpretation and is in need of interpretation. What counts as experience is neither self-evident nor straightforward; it is always contested, always therefore political. Experience, is, in this approach, not the origin of our explanation, but that which we want to explain. This kind of approach does not undercut politics by denying the existence of

> subjects, it instead interrogates the processes of their creation,
> and in so doing, refigures history and the role of the historian,
> and opens new ways for thinking about change (1992, p. 38).

Foundational concepts such as experience, woman, difference and identity cannot be abandoned, but they also cannot simply be accepted as they are presently constituted and deployed either. Rather than inhibit politics, the interrogation of these concepts illustrates how their construction, deployment and authorization is political.

Fuss uses the metaphor of a circle to describe the "authority of experience," in which some people are inside and some are outside. There are those "in the know," she says, "excluding and marginalizing those perceived to be outside the magic circle" (1989, p. 115). Only women have the authority to talk about women's experience, only Jews can talk about Jews, and only Blacks can talk about Blacks. There is a barrier that divides those who can know and those who cannot; and this sets up an identity politics based upon rigid exclusionary practices. Fuss's observation that when experience is exulted in the classroom some students are given a privileged platform and others are relegated to the sidelines, can be extended to any form of practice which centres on identity politics (1989, p. 115). In some settings, race and ethnicity "emerge as the privileged items of intellectual exchange," and in others sexual preference or gender will (p. 116). How do we attend to the problem of silencing the outsider? And how do we avoid the tendency to focus on and reduce people to one aspect of their identity — their malenesss, lesbianess or blackness where people are then expected to represent an entire diverse and heterogeneous community.

Identity politics adopts a moralism around who is entitled to speak about what and who is in the best social location to speak the truth. A hierarchy of oppression is produced in which, according to Linda Briskin, "the identification of certain oppressions as more salient than others promotes bonding on the bases of shared victimization, and exclusion organized around guilt, both of which undermine the possibility of political alliance between feminists" (1990, p. 105). Although the awareness of social diversity is a healthy and critical response to falsely universalized and exclusionary politics it is the "apolitical way in which identity is mobilized" that presents a problem (Briskin, p. 104). We must remember that gender and race are not simply identities they are systems of power.

Ilene Philipson characterizes identity politics in the following way:

> According to the proponents of a politics of identity, individuals
> in such a heterogeneous soceity have different experiences that

are ignored by a white, male, protestant ruling class. Therefore, the fundamental agenda of a politics of identity seeks respect for social diversity, greater inclusion, and representation. Implied in this is the assumption that if all identities were truly recognized as valid and fully represented politically, there would be little sustained criticism of our political system (1991, p. 51).

The ranking of identities authorizes certain people to speak on the "basis of truth of her lived experience," and refuses others the right to speak due to their lack of experience. In this process identities themselves are treated as fixed, immutable and exclusive. As Fuss suggests it then becomes possible to predict how someone will think or what they will say based on their identity. A major criticism of this trend in radical practice is that it is based upon inducing guilt in the other — it regulates and polices — "keeping the other in line." While it remains at the centre of feminist politics, feminist theorists are increasingly identifying the limitations of this approach as it focuses too much on the personal, on psychologizing, and tends to lose sight of "materialist analyses of the structural amd institutional bases of such exploitation" (Fuss, 1989, p. 117).

Identity politics are appealing to many though, as they emphasize the uniqueness of groups and provide analysis of particular oppression. While this trend in radical thought validates and affirms it does little organizing for social change. This attention to social diversity, greater inclusion and representation seems to suggest that if all identities were adequately recognized there would be little reason for social critique. Indeed, it can be argued that the focus on validation, and inclusion, disrupts the radical potential of identity groups.

But identity politics are seen to "stimulate personal awareness and political action" (Fuss, 1989, p. 97). Identity and essence are conflated, emphasizing "sameness, unity, and oneness. Group members are then seen to possess shared 'essences,' and a shared oppression" (p. 98). According to Fuss the relationship then between identity and politics is that "'we have an identity and therefore a politics. The link between identity and politics is causally and teleologically defined; for practitioners of identity politics, identity necessarily determines a particular kind of politics" (p. 99).

Identity politics is always reactionary, suggests Fuss, as it "fosters an apolitical amaterialist and subjectivist point of view" (1989, p. 100). The axioms "personal is political" and the "authority of experience" contribute to the development of identity politics. While the efforts were originally to legitimate the political aspects of personal life, feminism's increased focus on the personal has served to privatize oppression. Fuss, like others engaged in postmodern projects of problematizing theories of identity, recommends the necessity of bridging the notion of essence in identity with non-essentialized, discursive and non-stable multiplicity. Characterizing identity as contingent produces "a more mature identity politics by militating against the tendency to erase differences and inconsistencies in the production of stable political subjects" (Fuss, 1989, p. 104).

Postmodernism has made delineating difference its task when it needs to identify contradictions, tensions and layers of the ever-changing aspect of social identities. It is a paradoxically modernist flaw of postmodern emphasis on difference to construct our understanding of identity on the basis of opposition and dualism.

Focusing only on the other as different is as problematic as only focusing on sameness. Should we not go beyond simply producing the mirror image or precise opposite of that which we critique — itself a dualism or oppositional category? False unification or a focus on sameness obviously excludes, while a focus on difference tends to construct "aliens" or "others" (Bordo, 1990, p. 140). Moreover, differences between groups are too frequently essentialized, and differences within groups are negated.

Theresa De Lauretis queries the ironic postmodern tendency towards "reductive oppositions" (1985). In particular she questions the dualistic essentialism/anti-essentialism debate and the pitting of cultural and post-structuralist feminism against each other (p. 12). She believes that "either too much or too little is made of the "essentialism" imputed to most feminist positions (p. 4). Because essentialism has become a buzz-word it tends to no longer contribute to the elaboration of feminist theory. She advocates abandoning the essentialism/nominalism dualism, suggesting instead the category of woman and the understanding of a gendered subjectivity be seen as non-essentialised, and historical; that it is a position from which to ground the political (p. 11).

Pedagogically, and politically, it is possible to recognize diversity of experience and yet challenge people to explore how these experiences have been socially, historically and politically constructed. Exploring the construction of these experiences is in itself a way to politicize and change the limits of essentialism (Fuss, 1989, p. 119). Haug suggests that we need to attend to the paradoxes of experience in which experience is both an obstacle to and a necessary aspect of learning. That is, to understand that, "[e]xperiences are not simply truthful reflections and therefore as such possible foundations of learning processes. In experiences we can find the structures of this society and with them the results of processes of appropriation...and...that there is no possible learning process of any relevance which does not take up experiences" (1992, p. 4).

42

While postmodernism has contributed to the development of a new orientation for feminism and a new knowledge base for social work by its attention to the importance, for instance, of diversity and inclusion, postmodernism also has considerable weaknesses. Feminist postmodern theory has developed a certain prescriptiveness, legislating what can be considered adequate theory. Susan Bordo rejects the "methodologism" or authorative critical framework for theorizing identity as it forbids any generalizations about gender on theoretical grounds (1990, p. 135). It is doubtful, however, that all generalizations can be considered "pernicious universalization" (p. 138). This methodologism presumes that legislating a correct theoretical approach will make it possible to avoid ethnocentrism, to avoid the bias of one's own location.

Ironically, not unlike theories and practices based on identity politics, feminist postmodern theories also focus on intersecting race, class and gender in an attempt to recognize multiple identities. Thus, while feminist postmodernism rejects the essentialism of identity politics, it has often prescribed that good feminist theory must address the race, class, sex trilogy. Like its critique of identity politcs, postmodernism can be criticized for its reductionist and exclusionary approach to theory. Analysis needs to go beyond stating that race, class and sex intersect. While an analysis of women's oppression needs to be inclusive of multiple identities, one must question how many identity axes can be included in an analysis that still has focus or argument (Bordo, 1990).

Despite the emphasis on diversity in postmodern feminism, one can sense the desire to establish a cohesive wholeness comprising different parts. While feminist postmodernism objects to modernism's authoritativeness, it paradoxically legislates a "correct" and "incorrect" approach to theory and politics (Bordo, 1990, p. 135).

In addition to this authorativeness, feminist postmodernism also exemplifies some of the limitations of relativism. According to Susan Bordo, "to invoke the ideal of endless difference is for feminism either to self destruct or to finally accept an ontology of abstract individualism" (1990, p. 8). For Bordo the feminist pluralist dream of being everywhere is a new kind of detachment (p. 143). Bordo suggests the problem of postmodern relativism means "[refusing] to assume a shape for which one must take responsibility" (p. 144) and consequently, the postmodern emphasis on pluralism and heterogeneity has produced a "view from nowhere" (p. 137). A central question for Susan Bordo and other critics is, "how is the human knower to negotiate this infinitely perspectival, destabilized world" (p. 142)? The fantasy of transcending social location by acknowledging diversity or neutrality or detachment in modernist terms has just been replaced with a new version of detachment — the dream from everywhere. This somehow presumes that the knower can maintain a perspective of being able to see reality from all perspectives simply by wanting to. It is perhaps assumed that by recognizing social diversity one's own actual location no longer matters. This is simply a replacement, another mystification, another form of obscuring bias and location.

It is critical that feminism question the extent to which postmodernism advances social change, and to what extent it prohibits it. Its rejection of materialism, in favour of what seems an increasingly philosophically idealist thrust, may reflect an underlying conservatism within this paradigm. Postmodernism's ability to facilitate progressive social change for women is restricted by it focus on deconstruction rather than actual social change. Furthermore, the fragmentation which characterizes feminist postmodernism, and which arose through the attempt to deal with the pluralism of women's experiences, has itself demobilized political action. While contemporary feminism needs to move beyond critique, by revitalizing a vision of an alternative social world, postmodernism's opposition to totalizing theory will prohibit it from contributing to this development. There needs to be a shift in emphasis from theory and deconstruction to practice and change.

The elimination of social oppression and the advancement of social change are central guiding principles of feminist social work. Our political agenda is upfront and challenges the conventional methods of inquiry and knowledge production, which have often been accepted as objectified knowledge. Discovering how the oppressive conditions of people's lives are shaped and then working towards transforming these conditions cannot be achieved within the framework of conventional social work knowledge. Thus, feminist social work must abandon the hegemonic ideology which continually reproduces itself through social work pedagogy and practice. An emancipatory knowledge base and practice of social work must begin with an inclusive, non-universalized or essentialized understanding of the social world. Therefore, our efforts to embrace anti-sexist and anti-racist practice necessitate abandoning the "authority of experience," "politics of identity" and "hierarchy of oppression," which contribute to essentialism.

ENDNOTE

1. This essay builds on previous work including my Ph.D. comprehensive paper entitled, *Feminist therapy in the postmodern era: Epistemological and practical contributions to the women's movement.*

REFERENCES

Bordo, S. (1990). Feminism, postmodernism, and gender skepticism. In *Feminism/postmodernism*, ed. L. Nicholson, 133–156. New York: Routledge.

Briskin, L. (1990). Identity politics and the hierarchy of oppression: A comment. *Feminist Review* 35, Summer: 102–108.

Butler, J. (1992). Contingent foundations: Feminism and the question of 'postmodernism.' In *Feminists theorize the political*, eds. J. Butler and J. Scott, 3–21. New York: Routledge.

Butler, J. and J. Scott (eds.). (1992). *Feminists theorize the political.* New York: Routledge.

Crosby, C. (1992). Dealing with differences. In *Feminists theorize the political*, eds. J. Butler and J. Scott, 130–143. New York: Routledge.

De Lauretis, T. (1985). The essence of the triangle or, taking the risk of essentialism seriously: Feminist theory in Italy, the U.S., and Britain. *Differences* 1(2): 3–37.

Flax, J. (1990). Postmodernism and gender relations in feminist theory. In *Feminism/postmodernism*, ed. L. Nicholson, 39–62. New York: Routledge.

Fuss, D. (1989). *Essentially speaking. Feminism, nature and difference.* New York: Routledge.

Haug, F. (1992). Learning from experience. A feminist epistemology. Unpublished paper presented at the Ontario Institute for Studies in Education.

McLure, K. (1992). The issues of foundations: Scientized politics, politicized science, and feminist critical practice. In *Feminists theorize the political*, eds. J. Butler and J. Scott, 341–368. New York: Routledge.

Nicholson, L. (1990). *Feminism/postmodernism.* New York: Routledge.

Philipson, I. (1991). What's the big I.D.? The politics of the authentic self. *Tikkun*, November/December: 51–55.

Riley, D. (1988). *Am I that name? Feminism and the category of 'women' in history.* Minneapolis: University of Minnesota Press.

Scott, J. (1992). Experience. In *Feminists theorize the political*, eds. J. Butler and J. Scott, 22–40. New York: Routledge.

Smith, D. (1987). *The everyday world as problematic. A feminist sociology.* Toronto: University of Toronto Press.

Smith, D. (1990). *The conceptual practices of power. A feminist sociology of knowledge.* Toronto: University of Toronto Press.

CHAPTER 4

BORROWED KNOWLEDGE IN SOCIAL WORK: AN INTRODUCTION TO POST-STRUCTURALISM AND POSTMODERNITY

LINDSAY H. JOHN

INTRODUCTION

The use of borrowed knowledge in social work and other professions is common practice. That situation becomes problematic when particular professions see themselves as primarily consumers of knowledge and abrogate their responsibilities as generators of knowledge. Social workers, purportedly committed to critical thinking and political changes, are wont to ascribe to the arrival of a "paradigm shift" in the state of knowledge without being able to locate it. In other words, when pressed to articulate such an assertion, the usual reply is a definition of what Kuhn (1970) meant by the term "paradigm shift." I submit that the only conceptually radical shift in our conception of the foundation of knowledge, as it pertains to social work in particular and the social sciences in general, is occurring in the debates on postmodernity. The term postmodern, or companion terms postmodernity and postmodernism, are used to discuss a wide variety of phenomena in and claims about art, architecture, literature, philosophy, society and politics. Postmodernism is an epistemology with great relevance for social work, a profession purportedly committed to the welfare of citizens, inasmuch as it challenges the discipline's cherished assumptions about the nature of the "subject."

In the search for new knowledge one could examine various perspectives, distinguishing helpful from unhelpful insights. However, such a procedure is likely to make good sense only after at least an initial theoretical orientation is provided. My efforts in the following paragraphs will be directed predominantly to illuminate some ideas that will anchor the notion of postmodernity within a context of meaning relevant to social work. To understand the debates on postmodernity, one has to understand the relationship between the struturalist and post-structuralist theory of language. Once this relationship is understood, other closely related concepts, such as the strategies of deconstruction, will become evident. At this stage a caveat is in order. It cannot be stressed enough that any brief characterization of post-structuralism and postmodernity is a difficult task, inasmuch as these notions are a complex network of ideas and attitudes manifested in disciplines ranging from architecture through geography, to the very foundation of knowledge itself. Hence, my strategy will be to highlight some themes that appear to be of particular interest to social work epistemology at various levels of abstraction. The important question is: Does the emergence of a conceptual framework purporting to be a radical shift in the foundation of knowledge have any relevance for social work practices?

However, there is a point of controversy whether social work practices have an epistemological base in the philosophical sense of the word. I clearly recognize that there are various practices in the profession of social work, each anchored within a specific conceptual framework. They are based on whatever assumptions social workers ascribe to regarding the nature of individuals. However, they all share a common assumption, namely the well-being of individuals.

The following paragraphs are by no means a thorough review of the particularities of post-structuralism and postmodernity. The only claim is to identify the distinct and important innovations in the trajectory of the idea of postmodernity. In so doing the paper will attempt to give a clear and straightforward introduction to a range of work. The main objective is to examine the individual work of certain authors in their independent search for an epistemology not predicated on an absolutism anchored in the notion of the existence of an "objective reality." In other words, these authors have challenged the assumption that there is an objective reality in the universe that is waiting to be discovered by either the techniques of science or philosophical inquiry. A review of the separate efforts of these authors will reveal an internal coherence and overlap of work that is responsible for the way the concept of postmodernity is presently understood in academic circles. This article will not deal directly with the generalities of postmodernity. The article will deal instead with the conceptual foundation of postmodernity, namely the concept of post-structuralism. The topics of the present discussion are:

a. The relevance of the post-structuralist discourse for academic social work
b. The post-structuralist framework as the conceptual expression to the themes of the modernism/ postmodernism debate
c. The origins of the post-structuralist discourse
d. The worldview emerging from the post-structuralist discourse
e. The implication of that worldview for social work practices

THE RELEVANCE OF THE DISCOURSE FOR SOCIAL WORK

There is presently an important debate within the social scientific community — feminist practice, sociology, anthropology and social psychology — about the impact of postmodernist ideas on their respective disciplines. Insofar as social work considers itself to be an integral part of the social scientific community, it cannot either ignore or be complacent about such an ongoing debate. Yet, there is a manifest position within the discipline of social work that the deciphering of the ideas of postmodernity (or any new knowledge) is best left to the disciplines of psychology and sociology, and that once they have done the deciphering we can borrow their insights. Such a stance, I submit, is untenable. To adopt such a position is to assume a unitary purpose to all the social sciences. Notwithstanding some overlap with the precepts of other social sciences, we insist that our practice principles are somewhat unique. There is a propensity in the profession of social work to base programmatic theories on knowledge derived from other disciplines. Quite often the borrowed knowledge is introjected within our conceptual armamentarium without any thought given to its long-term effect on the structure and ethos of the profession. Furthermore, I take the position that, being an academic faculty, social work cannot abrogate its responsibility for debating and possibly assimilating knowledge from emerging conceptual frameworks. I am arguing not only for social work as a consumer but also as a generator of knowledge.

THE CHOICE OF THE POST-STRUCTURALIST FRAMEWORK

After much reading there is no doubt in my mind that the postmodern cannot be understood without a good grasp of the debates between the structuralist and post-structuralist conception of language. The postmodern is a condition that operates as if post-structuralism was true. There is a consensus among the actors engaged in the discursive context of postmodernity that the debate owes both its notoriety and intellectual respectability to the theories of post-structuralism (Easthope, 1991; White, 1991). By concentrating on post-structuralism, I not only avoid the controversy as to whether we are already in a postmodern era, but also avoid the "pop" aspects of postmodernism, for example: Is Madonna or Michael Jackson an embodiment of the postmodern entertainer? In fact the term postmodern has been grossly vulgarised in the mass media. The term has become so faddish that Foucault, a pioneer in the post-structuralist debate, when asked to comment on the idea of the postmodern, sardonically replied: "What are we calling postmodernity? I am not up to date" (Callinicos, 1990). In fact, to suggest that we are indeed manifestly in a postmodern era is to ignore the fact that periodization, i.e., the naming of an historical era, is usually the result of discursive convention (Hoesterey, 1991). In fact, one can seriously heed the tenets of post-structuralism and still by-pass the idea that we live in a postmodern epoch.

THE ORIGIN OF THE POST-STRUCTURALIST DISCOURSE

At its most basic level post-structuralism is a reaction to modernism. By modernism is meant those philosophical principles considered to be the foundation of knowledge. There is a consensus that the philosophical principles of modernism began with the tradition of rationality initiated by the philosophy of the Enlightenment (Ermarth, 1992; Descombes, 1987; Lyotard, 1984; Rorty, 1979). Hence, I will delineate the major assumptions of the Enlightenment and its parallel epistemology.

THE ENLIGHTENMENT

What is usually referred to as the Enlightenment is an eighteenth-century European philosophical movement characterized by rationalism, an impetus towards learning and a spirit of scepticism and empiricism in social and political thought (Angeles, 1981). One of its main proponents, the Marquis de Condorcet, viewed history as "the progress of the human mind" (Callinicos, 1990). According to Callinicos (ibid.), Condorcet saw this progress taking concrete shape in industrial society, where scientific knowledge would become the basis of social power and eradicate class antagonisms. These notions are referred to in the Frankfurt school of philosophy as the Enlightenment project, which is synonymous with the "project of modernity" (Habermas, 1987). Implicit in the so-called Enlightenment project is the concept of an ideal society towards which civilization might progress. Hence, Condorcet's conception that history is the "progress of the human mind" (Callinicos, 1990). The philosophy of enlightenment is predicated on two related assumptions, namely humanism and objective reality.

HUMANISM

Humanism is a philosophy that regards the rational individual as the highest value. It considers the individual to be the ultimate source of value, and is dedicated to fostering the individual's creative and moral development in a meaningful and rational way without reference to concepts of the supernatural (Angeles, 1981). Associated with humanism is the notion of a transcendental subject (self). Each individual possesses a unique essence of human nature, which in fact is rational consciousness. The subject is purported to be transcendental because it is endowed with a fundamental psyche that is not contingent on societal determination (Easthope, 1991). Within the philosophy of humanism the rational individual is at the centre of knowledge.

OBJECTIVE REALITY

Objective reality is simply the external reality to which our language and perceptions refer. The humanist conception of the transcendental, unified (centred) subject and the notion of an objective reality leads us to the notion of representational knowledge.

REPRESENTATIONAL KNOWLEDGE

This is the enlightenment view of philosophy, namely that the mind is conceived as a mirror that reflects the external objective reality (Rorty, 1979). It follows from that perspective that knowledge concerns itself with the accuracy of these reflections. Truth or meaning is seen as the correspondence between thought and language. Subjectivity is the coherent, authentic source of the interpretation of the meaning of "reality" (Weedon, 1987). The humanist conception of subjectivity refers to "a fundamental psyche which is prior to societal determination" (Easthope, 1991, p. 113).

As previously mentioned the project of the enlightenment is synonymous with the project of modernity. Modernity, characterized by the pursuit of a truth that has the character of absolute certainty, marks the inauguration of modern philosophy (Descombes, 1987). According to Descombes, it emerged when René Descartes undertook to reply to Montaigne's *Essays* with his *Discourse on Method.*

It may be useful to present the post-structuralists' position by presenting the major players and the positions they took about referential knowledge. In fact,

51

their attack on representational knowledge is the *sine qua non* of the post-structuralist position.

In keeping with the spirit of post-structuralism that there are no privileged referential points, the conceptual trajectory of the post-structuralist/postmodernity idea has many logical departure points. For example, one could begin with the peripheral players within the post-structuralist discourse. One could start with Marx's notion of the subject as constituted rather than constitutive. For students of political theory, Althusser and Balibar's (1975) reworking of Marx's notion of historical determinism and these authors' recognition that "there are different times in history" may be a fruitful departure point. Although now considered a peripheral player in the actual post-structuralist discourse, Althusser nevertheless provided one of the better critiques of "essentialism," which embraces all epistemologies that oppose a given subject to a given object and call knowledge the abstraction by the subject of the essence of the object (Easthope, 1988). According to Easthope (ibid.), the major influence on British post-structuralism was Althusser. Another philosopher whose ground-breaking work on the philosophy of language ultimately contributed to a shift towards post-structuralism was Ludwig Wittgenstein. He based his later philosophical work on the primacy of language and its groundlessness. Whereas Wittgenstein's work is considered to be a philosophy of language, the structuralism of Ferdinand de Saussure is considered a linguistic theory. Wittgenstein's philosophy was an attack on the "Cartesian model of the mind as some distinct container, or closet, in which peculiarly 'mental' experiences, ideas or meanings are harbored" (Barrett, 1978, p. 69). To Wittgenstein "the meaning of a word has to do with the way we use it within the total web of our discourse" (Barrett, ibid., p. 69). Hence, within such a discursive context, language is not a pointer to things that purportedly exist in objective reality. Although it could be argued that no substantial grasp of post-structuralist philosophy can be attempted without an understanding of Wittgenstein and Althusser, my preference is to start with the notion of structuralism as exemplified in the work of the linguist Ferdinand de Saussure.

In fact, the post-structuralist discourse starts with the structural linguistics of Ferdinand de Saussure in the early part of this century. The linguistic structuralism of Saussure was the first to challenge representational knowledge. His basic premises were: language, far from reflecting an objective reality, constitutes reality for us; neither social reality nor the 'natural' world has fixed intrinsic meanings, which language reflects or expresses (Weedon, 1987), in other words, meaning is not to be understood by analysing the relationship of words to their referents (i.e., things in the world) but by tying meaning more to the relationship of signs to one another (White, 1991). Saussure theorized language as an abstract system consisting of chains of signs. Each sign is made up of a signifier (sound or written image) and a signified (meaning) (Descombes, 1987). The two components of the sign are related to each other without any natural connection between the sound image and the concept it identifies. The feminist writer Chris Weedon (1987) gave a good example of what is meant by that statement. For example, it is not anything intrinsic to the signifier "whore" that gives it its meaning, but rather its difference from other signifiers of womanhood such as "virgin," "wife," "mother," etc.

Within the framework of linguistic theory, Saussure assumed that meaning is made possible by the existence of an underlying system of conventions and not as pointing to reality (Weedon, 1987). Meaning is constituted within language and is not guaranteed by the subject who speaks it. Another way of expressing this is that the origin of meaning can no longer be located in the individual who believes he or she is expressing himself or herself, but rather that it lies in language itself (Weedon, 1987). Within language "subject and object come into existence together, in a reciprocally situated relation" (Easthope, 1991, p. 19). What makes a client "emotionally disturbed" is not the rational mind of the therapist assessing an objective reality which inheres in the client. In post-structuralist terms, both client and therapist are said to be resident in the discursive context of the "pathological model."

The problem with Saussure's linguistics, according to the post-structuralists, is that he insisted on a pre-given structuring of language prior to its realization in speech. For example, Saussure assumed that meaning and signification are both transparent and already in place (Weedon, 1987). He attempted to locate meaning in the language system itself but then saw it as 'fixed.' The term structuralism implies that there is a structure to language that is absolute, hence universal. According to Easthope (1991), implicit in structuralism is the claim that its structure has an objective reality that could become the object of scientific knowledge. Hence, stucturalism moves us beyond representational knowledge but not beyond essentialism.

Saussure's linguistics does not account for the plurality of meaning or historical changes in meaning. If Saussure's linguistics was the first sustained attack on representational knowledge, the major sustained attack on the essentialism of Saussure's linguistics was that of Jacques Derrida. Derrida is associated most closely with post-structuralism precisely because he was the first to investigate and expose the contradictions and paradoxes upon which structuralism is formed (Norris, 1987). It was Derrida who questioned the location of social meaning in fixed signs. Derrida's work is fundamentally a drawn-out, sustained attack on the possibility of there being transcendental points of reference (Percesepe, 1989). Derrida denied the very possibility of literal meaning. This is because the literal assumes the absolute self-presence of meaning (Weedon, 1987). The very notion of transcendental points of reference is at the core of the post-structuralist attack on the assumptions of modernity. At this point I want to introduce two terms of post-structuralism: intertextuality (Derrida) and discourse (Foucault).

Derrida's conception of intertextuality means that every text[1] is penetrated with traces of other texts so that neither is the single text itself the ultimate locus of meaning, nor does the author determine the meaning of the text (Doherty, Graham and Malek, 1992). Thus language, the language of intertextuality, becomes the focal concern (Norris, 1987). To go into Derrida's post-structuralist particularities is beyond the present discourse; his work is the most obtuse of the post-structuralist writings. However, what needs to be stated here is that it is Derrida who is most closely associated with the notion of deconstruction. The latter is a term that has been in ascendance in the social sciences over the last decade or so. Basically, Derrida's idea of deconstruction is the dismantling of the fixed conceptual oppositions as is to be found in the structuralism of Saussure. Deconstruction is the deconstructing of the status of foundational, meaning-endowing oppositions of structuralism. Derrida's strategy of deconstruction was to show that the claimed essentialism of structuralism "collapses or undermines itself when thought through" (White, 1991, p. 15). Deconstruction is a method of grasping the "unwritten" in texts. It is a method of reading text with its own specific rules and protocols (Norris, 1987). It is the careful teasing out of the biases, defined by normative consensus, of the accepted Western mode of thinking, of the contradictory aspects of signification within the text itself. According to Percesepe (1989), if anything is destroyed in a deconstructive reading, it is not the text but the claim to unequivocal domination of one mode of signifying over another.

Whereas Derrida insists that no meaning exists outside the text, Michel Foucault introduces the notion of "discourse" that implies the political aspects of the discursive context. However, Derrida's work pointed to a different direction; instead, he argued that the political dimensions were merely species of naïve referential delusion (Norris, 1987). To Foucault, discourse was the missing element in Saussure's dualism of signified and signifier. Foucault's strategy was "to explore not only these discourses but also the will that sustains them and the strategic intention that supports them" (Foucault, 1990, p. 8). Although Foucault's work is the one that I believe has the most relevance for the social sciences, it is the hardest to grasp. My understanding of his argument is that analysis of discourse is a task that consists of not treating discourses as groups of signs (signifying elements referring to content or representation) but as practices that systematically form the objects of which they speak (Foucault, 1983). Of course, discourses are composed of signs, but what they do is *more* than use these signs to designate things. It is this *more* that renders them irreducible to language and to speech. It is this *more* that must be revealed and described (Weedon, 1987). The *more*, to Foucault, comprises all the discursive rules and categories that are an *a priori* constituent and formative part of any discourse, and so fundamental to its existence that they remain unvoiced and unthought (Weedon, ibid.). To Foucault (Hoy, 1986), meaning is to be located in the totality of the discursive context, which includes historically derived conventional rules. In other words, meaning always takes the forms defined for it by historically specific discourses. Discourses are ways of constituting knowledge together with social practices, forms of subjectivity and power relations that inhere in such knowledge and the relations between them (Foucault, 1983). The ways in which discourses constitute the minds and bodies of individuals (subjectivity) are always part of a wider network of power relations, often with institutional bases. Subjectivity occurs through the identification by the individual with particular subject positions within discourses (Weedon, 1987). While a discourse will offer a preferred form of subjectivity, its very organization will imply other subject positions and the possibility of reversal (Weedon, ibid).

In summary, both Derrida and Foucault, their disagreements on method notwithstanding, stressed the fragmentary, heterogeneous and plural character of reality. Furthermore, they both denied the rational consciousness of the subject of humanist philosophy the ability to arrive at any objective account of that reality (Callinicos, 1990).

THE MOOD OF POSTMODERNISM

According to Dews (1987), the post-structuralist writings of the sixties have moved in the eighties towards what we now refer to as postmodernism. The shortest description of postmodernism is by Jean-François Lyotard: "incredulity towards metanarratives" (Lyotard, 1984). Metanarratives are those foundational interpretive schemes that have constituted the sources for the justification of scientific, technological and political projects in the modern world. Such narratives, focusing on God, nature, progress and emancipation, are to Lyotard the anchors of modern life. That incredulity is, in a sense, more or less a resistant state of mind, shared by academicians and lay people alike who feel dominated by and hence resist the way modern metanarratives represent reality (Easthope, 1991). Lyotard is probably the most influential writer to have converged the writings of post-structuralism and the various aspects of post-industrial society into a coherent argument. The major tenet of his *magnum opus, The Postmodern Condition* (1984), is a refutation of the existence of any transcendental frame of reference under which notions of a grand theory or a just society can be subsumed. Like his post-structuralist predecessors, Lyotard is anti-foundational, i.e., opposed to the dogma of universality. Lyotard's work is a complex network of ideas and attitudes that converge in a discourse of emancipation. The assumption of linear progress in society is challenged. In fact, modernity and modern reason are viewed as inherently repressive. The postmodern, to Lyotard, envisages a radically heterogeneous society with no central value structure. Even though postmodernity stresses relativity, instability and indeterminacy of meaning, it is not a philosophy of nihilism. The possibility of rationally mediating reality is never denied. A postmodern epistemology is one where the pursuit of knowledge is carried out without the need to adopt a deterministic referential point. Again, like post-structuralism, postmodernism challenges the humanist subject. Postmodernity decentres the subject. In other words, the subject is no longer the primary focus of interest or activity.

What then is the origin of the incredulity towards metanarratives? To state it differently: Why has the optimism of belief in the project of modernity, as a project of continuous enlightenment, entered a crisis? To the postmodernists the answer is simple — because we cannot place such confidence in human works as we have done in the past. For example, there is no evidence that scientific progress is associated with an emancipation of people towards a better world. The promise of continuous enlightenment is confuted by major, socially created calamities like senseless wars, genocide and urban decay.

Habermas, the main proponent of the project of modernity, wants to rehabilitate the project of modernity by positing it as incomplete (Habermas, 1987). Habermas's plea is to give the project of modernity more time since, according to him, human nature is steadily progressing towards moral improvement (Habermas, ibid.). Habermas sees the post-structuralist position as "a discourse of irrationality poised to displace the tradition of rationality" (Habermas, ibid.). To the post-structuralists, the dispute about modernity is not a dispute about reason or the possibility of human enlightenment but one about its narrow conception and illusory aspects of its foundational premises (White,1991).

THE MAIN TENETS OF THE POST-STRUCTURALIST'S WORLDVIEW AND IMPLICATIONS FOR SOCIAL WORK PRACTICES

The challenge of the post-structuralist position can be taken up by the profession of social work at various levels of abstraction. An exhaustive delineation of such possibilities is not what the present argument is all about. The intent of the preceding discussion is to provide an introduction to interested social workers to the main arguments that frame the post-structuralist/ postmodernity debates. Obviously, there are endless implications for social work practices that can be deduced from these debates. For example, at the most pragmatic level we could heed Sands and Nuccio (1992) that "the use of deconstruction to uncover the suppressed voice of marginalized populations provides a means through which social workers can work in concert with client groups to promote social change" (p. 493). To this writer, the most profound challenge of post-structuralist principles to social work practice is twofold.[2] The first is the post-structuralist challenge to the idea of the sovereignty of the subject. The second is the challenge to representational knowledge. In relation to the first challenge we have to realise that our most cherished notion of self-determination is predicated on the humanist conception of the subject as the freely choosing and constitutive individual. The post-structuralist view of subjectivity is not the unified rational subject of humanism, but subjectivity as characterized by conflict and disunity subject to historically specific discourses. The challenge to social work theoreticians is the need to grasp the implication of Foucault's (1983) notion of subjectivity as the site of consensual regulation of individuals. As practitioners we need to become cognizant of the fact that clients enact particular subject roles within the discursive context of therapy. The object of the therapeutic enquiry, therefore, must be grounded in reflexivity. By reflexivity is meant our awareness of our place as helpers in the discursive context of therapy. In other words, we need to be aware of the discursive logic of our practice. We need to understand the interplay of the language that is used by client and therapist. We, as well as the client, are a function of the logic of language. The problem-solving practices we have acquired as a profession obviously have provided us with a set of prescriptions to practise our trade. These prescriptions, like the play of signs within language, shape our attitudes and perceptions of the client and hence dictate the discursive context of our practice. It follows then, that it is important that we attempt to localize the genealogy of our practice principles.

The second challenge of post-structuralism to social work practices is the challenge to representational knowledge. The post-structuralist rejection of a concept of "truth" waiting to be discovered marks the end of "enquiry" and its replacement by "conversation" (Doherty, Graham and Malek, 1992). The therapeutic encounter, when conceived within the logic of the pathological model, underscores the importance of enquiry. The enquiry usually leads to a diagnosis or a conceptual formulation. The implication of post-structuralism for that type of practice means the abandonment of explanatory psychological theories of personality or theories of psychopathology. To reiterate, in post-structuralism there is no fundamental psyche that is prior to societal determination. Therefore we must try not so much to understand the personality dynamics of the client but rather to attempt to grasp the totality of the discursive context of his or her predicaments. In that sense, at least, social work practice principles converge with the tenets of post-structuralism. Parenthetically, one wonders whether social work's ecological model of clients' predicaments can be expanded to accommodate the notions of both discourse and intertextuality. As a profession we have always believed that there is conceptual value in attending to the ordinary accounts people give us about their predicaments. The object of the client/worker encounter is shared social knowledge rather than the uncovering of private individual mental processes (Doherty, Graham and Malek, ibid.). Clients' accounts of their predicaments have the function of making sense as a process and not as data for later categorization. The primacy of process over content has always had an axiomatic quality in social work. Furthermore, research on the therapeutic alliance between client and therapist has cast great doubt on the usefulness of specific theoretical traditions as a contributing factor in the healing process. There are many effective social workers who feel that they have no need for transcendental theoretical justification for systematizing their practice principles.

As a concluding remark, I want to stress that the previous discussion was an attempt to introduce to social work practitioners, albeit in an elementary form, the idea of postmodernity and its antecedents. I believe that whether or not we adopt the post-structuralist view of the world, we may be ethically responsible to teach new recruits to the profession the importance of language in shaping our perception of both the therapeutic encounter and our clients.

ENDNOTES

1. The term "text" in the post-structuralist discourse is used in an expanded version which includes artifacts ranging from architecture, books, events, theories etc.(Hoesterey, 1992)
2. When I refer to social work practices I am referring to the client/worker dyad, as it is the practice I am most familiar with.

REFERENCES

Althusser, L. and E. Balibar. (1975). *Reading capital.* London: New Left Books.

Barrett, W. (1979). *The illusion of technique.* London: Willam Kimber.

Callinicos, A. (1990). *Against postmodernism: A Marxist critique.* New York: St Martins Press.

Deleuze, G. (1988). *Foucault.* London: Athlone.

Descombes, V. (1989). *Modern French philosophy.* Cambridge: Cambridge University Press.

Dews, P. (1987). *Logic of disintegration: Post-structuralist thought and the claims of critical theory.* London: Verso.

Doherty, J., E. Graham and M. Malek. (1992). *Postmodernism and the social sciences.* New York: St Martins Press.

Easthope, A. (1991). *British post-structuralism since 1968.* London: Routledge.

Ermarth, E. D. (1992). *Sequel to history: Postmodernism and the crisis of representational time.* Princeton: Princeton University Press.

Foucault, M. (1990). *The history of sexuality. Volume 1: An introduction.* New York: Vintage Books.

Habermas, J. (1987). *The philosophical discourse of modernity: Twelve lectures.* Cambridge: MIT Press.

Hoesterey, I. (1991). *Zeitgeist in Babel: The postmodernist controversy.* Bloomington: Indiana University Press.

Hoy, D. C. (1986). *Foucault: A critical reader.* New York: Basil Blackwell.

Lyotard, J. (1984). *The postmodern condition: A report on knowledge.* Minneapolis: University of Minnesota Press.

Norris, C. (1987). *Derrida.* Cambridge: Harvard University Press.

Percesepe, G. J. (1989). *Future(s) of philosophy: The marginal thinking of Jacques Derrida.* New York: Peter Lang.

Rorty, R. (1979). *Philosophy and the mirror of nature.* Princeton: University of Princeton Press.

Sands, R. G., and K. Nuccio. (1992). Postmodern feminist theory and social work. *Social Work* 37(6): 489–494.

Weedon, C. (1987). *Feminist practice and poststructuralist theory.* Oxford: Blackwell.

White, S. (1991). *Political theory and postmodernism.* Cambridge: Cambridge University Press.

CHAPTER 5

POSTMODERNITY AND SOCIAL WORK DISCOURSE(S): NOTES ON THE CHANGING LANGUAGE OF A PROFESSION

ADRIENNE S. CHAMBON

One day in Chicago in the mid-80s, I stumbled upon the uncritical importing of discourse into the field of social work. Frank Breul, then editor of the *Social Service Review*, sharply rebuked me for stating that "X will impact on social work." "How can you of all people say something like that?" he exclaimed. Taking the look of bewilderment on my face as naïve ignorance, he proceeded to explain that the use of "impact" as a verb has its origins in military discourse; however, he claimed, its increasing use in social work was antithetical to the mission of our profession and further, he added, he would not tolerate it.

PROFESSIONAL DISCOURSE(S) AND THE STATE OF THE ART

One way to reflect upon the signs of change occurring in a professional or academic field is to examine the language of its professional claims (Bloom, Wood and Chambon, 1991). This entails not simply examining the specific content of prioritized topics, i.e., the changing list of "welfare problems of concern" as traditional content analysis would, but instead highlighting what is called its "discourse" (Potter and Wetherell, 1987; Ricoeur, 1976), i.e., the structuring of thought obtained through specific patterns of language which constitute its dominant cognitive schemata and cut across diverse content areas.

The exploration of professional language-in-use makes explicit what Dorothy Scott (1989) has referred to as "meaning construction," or the internalized frames of reference and socially constructed intersubjective meanings shared by participants in a profession (see also Rodger, 1991). Construction, in this sense, links theory to practice and policy arenas. For Murray Edelman (1988) the ways in which we define social problems are closely connected to the dominant assumptions and values of our professional field and, in turn, to the specific range of "viable" solutions which we contemplate. Foucault (1974) has convincingly argued that changing forms of legitimation follow a historical process, as particular interpretive maps and systems of categorization come to be replaced by others. There is no expectation that a single unitary discourse be hegemonic in any field of activity at a particular point of time, but rather that dominant patterns and trends can be identified.

Current writings on social work and postmodernism have tended to situate social work as being in an uncertain transition towards postmodernism, held back by conventional forms of thinking (Sands and Nuccio, 1992). Focusing on the conceptual and epistemological transformations of the field, these authors herald an alternative knowledge base in social work and modified positions/relations between professionals and clients — a project that can be achieved by incorporating post-structuralist and feminist frameworks, resulting in a major revision of social work premises (also Gorman, 1993). From a philosophical standpoint, Renaud (1991) stresses the failure of the rationalistic and normalizing project of human relations orchestrated by the welfare state and social service institutions and embraces more shifting, decentred, less rational positions for clients and professionals. Others, such as McBeath and Webb (1991), engaged in the debate from an organizational and structural point of view, bear witness to the swift changes currently transforming the social service arena. They argue that already we are deeply entrenched in the postindustrial age, cautioning us against the economic and institutional arrangements that accompany such trends. This paper is situated differently. It is an attempt to step back and consider a number of the more innovative practices of our professional field, in the light of trends and dilemmas, through a form of discursive reading.

I will attempt to illuminate the place of social work in a postmodern environment and its contribution to postmodernity by examining (a) the emerging terminology and labelling activity of our profession, or the words we use and their related discursive effects, and (b) the dominant narratives and narrative structures in the field of social work. This approach is in keeping with my current work on discourse and methodology (Chambon, 1993; Chambon and Bellamy, in press). In a postmodern spirit, fragments and bits of observations will be presented and expanded into lines of questioning. These comments are intended to stimulate reflexiveness upon our societal position, which is to be distinguished from reflectiveness or the thoughtful examination of practice.

THE MULTIPLICATION AND SPLINTERING OF EXPERTISE

I will refer in this section to the development of specialized areas around problems, skills, approaches, models and restricted bases of knowledge.

The proliferation of social work journals, as much as it corresponds to the expansionist market of academic journals in all disciplines and the spin-off of specialized author/readerships, reflects and amplifies the multiplication of expert domains within the field of social work. The older established journals — *Social Work, Social Service Review* and *Social Casework* — were generic in nature. An intermediary period saw the development of journals differentiated according to institutional arrangements and practices — *Health and Social Work, Clinical Journal of Social Work, Social Work with Groups.* An increasingly narrower focus characterizes social work journals established in the last ten years, as their titles indicate: *Child and Adolescent Social Work Journal* (1984), the *Journal of Health and Social Policy* (1989), *Affilia: Women and Social Work* (1986), the *Journal of Multicultural Social Work* (1991) or the *Journal of Independent Social Work* (1987). Clearly, publications in social work participate in the increasing partitioning of information into discrete areas of expertise; a trend that can be expanded without limits other than the market.

To their credit, a number of these new outlets legitimize a space of debate for previously marginalized voices (women, racial and ethnic minorities). This is not the case, however, for most of these new ventures. A potentially questionable outcome of this trend, which needs consideration, is the promotion of restricted spaces of knowledge as self-contained objects. Unlike the more traditional branching off into new fields of knowledge that characterizes the emergence of new disciplines, the recent multiplicity is a plurality of closed objects, rather than avenues of inquiry. Positions are being conquered while no new field is being created.

One such area of expertise is the growing domain of ethics, which used to unify social workers under the common banner of a professional code of ethics. Along with other fields (i.e., Sisela Bok, 1982), it has recently taken on a life of its own with recognized experts (i.e., Abramson, 1985; Reamer, 1982; 1989), while the rest of us become defined as unexperts by default. The development of domains of expertise, which strive to become sources of authority and legitimation (Illich, 1978), is not a new trend, but it can have negative implications if it is not critically examined. The discussion of ethics, with its selective emphasis on the advancement of multiple arenas of application, its identification of critical decision points in action and the privileged inquiry into ethical pragmatics and legal competencies, is not accompanied by a debate on the premises of such a knowledge base and its underlying philosophy. Limited examination is made of the priority given to individualistic vs. collective ethics, or the immense attention paid to the legal ramifications of ethics reviews, consent forms and malpractice suits. A pointed-application approach to knowledge specialization obliterates more unitary forms of inquiry.

Social work theories also are multiplying. In the clinical field, "attachment theories" (e.g. McMillen, 1992; Sable, 1992; Schneider, 1991), "self psychology" and "object relations" fill in the theoretical space at an unprecedented speed, with a corresponding abundance of workshops and training packages. This exponential growth takes place within a combinatory logic framework so that separate considerations given to feminist perspectives and to addictions, can be regrouped into a brand new interest entitled: "Feminist perspective on addictions" — as a recent title by Springer Publications indicates. Combinations follow permutations and a title such as "Women as therapists" can be complemented by the symmetrical label of "Women managers" — both titles by the same publisher. In a structural sense (postmodernity was coeval with the development of post-structuralism), this combinatory property holds true for any topic. Any activity can be constructed using this principle: "Feminism + ethics + mental health" would yield "feminist ethics in psychiatry." These new interests function as so many fragmented narratives of expertise or referential intersections, automatically generating boundless needs for knowledge consumption. There lies the combinatory appeal of "eclecticism" as a postmodern trend. This in turn will lead consumers and producers of knowledge in direct service, but also in research to a continuous quest, keeping abreast of more recent developments, maintaining an adequate level of competency through ever faster mechanisms of updating and upgrading.

Our principal concern with the fragmentation of social welfare problems is parallel to that expressed by McBeath and Webb (1991) for whom an increasing trend towards specialization, fragmentation and "determinate dispersal" is closely connected to a managerial and technocractic ideology of segmented performance and efficiency. From a knowledge standpoint, such a direction leaves little room for examining the sources and commonalities of these problems and the broader social conditions against which they are produced. New knowledge does not necessarily entail reflexive thought. We run a grave risk of using the newly coined terms in an uncritical manner.

The ever-growing terminology of family violence, for instance, is used mostly to characterize family relations and does not include manifestations of institutional violence, which lie outside its parameters of inquiry. There is no equivalent concept to characterize the violent impact of social dislocation, loss of employment, "restructuration" (or the more recent "modernization") of the economy, lack of access to health or housing, or the impact of symbolic violence such as stereotyping and labelling (Mirowski and Ross, 1983). In summary, the splintering of expertise entails a very real hazard of uncritical conceptual fragmentation.

SOCIAL WELFARE PROBLEMS AND MEDIA-LED IMAGERY

A striking resemblance, if not close correspondence, can be found between the representation of social problems in the media and the definition of social problems in social work. Urgent problems such as AIDS, homelessness or sexual abuse are similarly represented in these distinct fields. A commonsensical argument is that this signals social work's commitment to the problems of our time and the development of practice and its theoretical base in keeping with current issues.

This affinity of perspective can alternatively be thought of as deeply troubling. This phenomenon can be interpreted, in Baudrillard's terminology, as a manifestation of the "prismatic" effect of media imagery onto other fields of knowledge, the privileging of simulation over the real and even of simulation standing as the real (Baudrillard, 1983; Poster, 1988).

As various problem areas become fashionable and worthy of attention, the strength of visual imagery as "spectacle" (Debord, 1967; Edelman, 1988) plays a central role through its argumentative appeal. The beauty of images enthralls and entraps us; and this includes images of violence. We are "seduced" by certain images, and through aesthetic replay we simultaneously fail to reflect on their construction. In the U.S., for instance, the emphasis on the use of cocaine by the black population, until recently, negated the statistical evidence according to which the white population constitutes its predominant user. This distortion held true for the media as well as for social work. Social work thus carries forward images, uncritically importing them from other fields of activity.

As an illustration, social workers tend to prioritize certain ethnic groups while disregarding others. The needs of the Somali community in Toronto have been extensively discussed in the media (both Canadian and U.S.), and consistent with this image (associated with traditional dress and war clippings from Somalia), this community has become a priority target group for research. The Somali community are justifiably at the centre of existing research on child, family and housing issues and refugee populations. However, this emphasis dismisses the repeated assertions made by community leaders according to whom other African groups are more numerous locally and in just as great a need (i.e., Ghanaian) — a point emphasized to us in a network we instituted at the Faculty of Social Work with representatives from various new immigrant communities.

65

Yet, they remain inexplicably absent from the media and from academic and professional debates. Thus, disadvantaged and oppressed groups are differentially included and excluded from a discourse on legitimate needs. It appears as if selected images "stick" and are imported into the discourse of social work, while others remain conspicuously missing.

The logic of the media becomes intertwined with that of economic interests to further legitimize a selective agenda. Sources of funding for service delivery and for research activities establish competitive arenas around selected, high-profile issues. As academics become increasingly dependent on outside funding for knowledge development, university departments of social work become reactive to this agenda setting and framing of problems in particular ways. Social workers tend to adopt these legitimate images, further contributing to their own legitimation in a circular logic.

The interventionist field of social work can be thought of as a running commentary on society at a given point in time. In the present context, social workers have become strange bedfellows with other commentators and, in particular, are adopting uncontrolled and unmediated media-led messages. The questions we need to ask ourselves are the following: Are we producing knowledge responsibly or heteronomically reproducing the terms of other institutions' agendas, thus furthering consensual understanding? What is guiding our agenda? Should we, and can we, as a profession, construct our own autonomous agenda and interpellate others ?

COMMODIFICATION OF SOCIAL WORK KNOWLEDGE

Against the prevailing mode of dependency and fragmentation, social work has maintained some metanarratives while claiming that this vision is no longer realistic: "A great unifying theory theoretical panacea is not going to emerge.... We are much more comfortable with the prospect of being multitheoretical in our practice" (Turner, 1986, p. 646). Systems theory is still alive with its holistic reading of complex "people-environment interactions." A remnant of modernity, it has been maligned for its dullness and lack of response to diversity. Its proponents have responded by elaborating reified concepts and the packaging of crisp professional tools such as "the ecomap," "the genogram" (1985) and the by-now necessary software package for clinical practice, "Visual Ecoscan" — developed under the auspices of the National Association of Social Workers in both IBM-PC and MacIntosh versions. These packages contribute to the technological and visual imperatives of legitimate social work activity.

Social workers are actively engaged in a competitive quest for models and maps which provide practice guidelines and solutions, periodically replaced by new users' manuals. These guidelines tend to be proposed as commodities ready for consumption, and are correspondingly removed from an historical and reflective understanding of their development and implementation. Yet, a model is but a moment in knowledge development, a point of closure which does not generate new questions.

Narratives do not escape such a transformational process and can be stilted once submitted to a process of modelization. To be convincing and to add to my credibility, I gave my own programme of research — Narrative Strategies of Telling and Talking (N.S.T.T.) — which serves as a handle, a label, possibly a copyright protection. In this, like others, I "sell" my way of thinking. Funders and publishers operate similarly in supporting this approach. We become consultants for our own thinking. The process of commodification of thought and knowledge acts as a screen, an illusion of grasp — there may be more than a minor problem at playing this game unwittingly. Such products fail to accommodate the permanence of social conflict or even the distribution of social positions.

TERMINOLOGY: BETWEEN HIGH CULTURE AND LOW CULTURE

Social work imports a terminology not just imagery. The accepted terminology of social work is always at a difficult crossroads as it accommodates a diversity of logics and languages into a single professional field (Bloom, Wood and Chambon, 1991). Historically, the clinical domain of social work has borrowed concepts from the field of psychiatry, such as the concept of "diagnosis" and more commonsensical references such as the key notion of "person-environment."

A more recent notion like that of "co-dependency," used in popular literature to characterize family relations, particularly in the context of substance abuse, can also be found in the professional literature. This notion is not quite a lay term, nor is it a full-fledged concept. As a quasi-scientific descriptor of an interpersonal dynamic, its usage manifests the thin distinction currently existing between popular culture and social work. Part of this fuzziness lies in the blurred audiences of professionals writing for broad audiences beyond the confines (and limited financial rewards) of professional and academic circles. Theoretical constructs "leak" into ordinary language, and popular language is imported into the professional/academic field of social work without redefinition.

At the other end of the spectrum, the aesthetic language of upper-class social work practice is equally striking. Family therapists use increasingly separate terminologies; in earlier times, systems concepts were derived from cybernetics. More recent additions, such as the language of "chaos," are an attempt to link

67

highly skilled social work practitioners to the abstract worlds of physical science and the humanities. Such terminology is restricted to an elite, the more psychoanalytically inclined practitioners, and family therapists. It is a language of aesthetic slogans and belonging, participation in cultural images and class demarcation. Who speaks that language, and what is the effect of speaking it? This is yet another example of the discursive segmentation of the field.

The Language of Management

More strikingly, the language of management has become a dominant mode of expression in social work. Yet, at the onset, the logics of the two fields would tend to locate them at polar ends. When their discourses become one and the same, it leads us to wonder about the current autonomy of social work. A striking example of the adoption of management language by social workers is the modified title of one of its long-standing and established journals, *Social Casework*, which became *Families in Contemporary Society* in 1990. The traditional pivotal notion of "casework" was displaced in favour of an updated family-oriented name. It is worth noting that in the U.S., where the change originated, family terminology is easily legitimized, positively connoted from a range of social perspectives.

This change conveys the idea that the notion of "casework" has faded out. Indeed, its replacement by the widely used concept of "case management" indicates a remarkable change of direction. The concept of "work" is still present in the core identity terms of "social work" and "social worker." However, case management as the central rational activity of social work has become the object of a growing body of literature. The *Journal of Case Management* was established in 1992 with an identifiable audience; and numerous books are being published on the topic (i.e., *Case management in human service practice*, Jossey-Bass, 1985; *Social work case management*, Aldine de Gruyter, 1992).

This substitution of labels is indicative of a real social transformation. The mission of social work seems to have become confused with its organizational and institutional arrangements. As professionals conduct the legitimate activity of case management, the language of management becomes incorporated into the social work profession. Such a permeability of boundaries is in sharp contrast to the previous confrontation of the field to its institutional constraints and conditions for survival, the conflict between professional values and bureaucratic demands — traditionally presented in social work education as one of the core dilemmas of the helping profession (i.e., Compton and Gallaway, 1984).

The advertisement to the 1990 supplement of the *Encyclopedia of Social Work* highlights new entries in problem areas (AIDS, violence, homelessness, genetics) and innovations in service delivery, specifically "case management," "the business of social work" and "marketing" a coherent set of items. Further, as case management denotes short-term intervention, the new term of "long-term management" has been coined to replace what was previously thought of as a clinical social work activities. The domain of the "clinical" is seemingly becoming subsumed under a managerial logic.

Technological language complements this orientation. Concepts such as "egosyntonic," "feedback loops" and "interface" are increasingly objects of casual use. In keeping with the times, social workers currently employ the language of computers, artificial intelligence and information processing. However, there are some unintended effects in these implementations. A phrase such as "give me feedback" comes to substitute for the utterance "let's talk;" "how do you process this?" replaces "how do you make sense of this?" A linguistic reading of this newspeak shows the transformation from substantive forms to verbal state forms, i.e., the use of the notion of "interface" is increasingly used in its verbal form, as in the statement: "let's interface" — which stands for exchanging ideas and impressions. As argued by the linguist Michael Halliday (1973), indeed, "the syntax enunciates the theme."

The restricted languages of technology and management convey a paradoxical message in the context of a helping profession, which traditionally placed the helping relationship at the centre of its activity. By contrast, the new technological language is "cool" (Baudrillard in Poster, 1988) and remote. We no longer "feel," instead we "emote." It is a language of the surface of things (vs. depth), characterized, as Jameson (1984) puts it, by a "flatness" and "waning of the affect." The intransitive verbal forms, "clients emote" and "social workers liaise" (instead of making referrals and establishing linkages), convey a connective superficiality in the discourse of interpersonal relations.

Out of compensation, some of the more popular clinical theories today are the theories of attachment. There is a growing interest for the notion of "caring" (i.e., Imre, 1990); some figures in the field recommend exploring the link between social work and spirituality (Canda, 1991). These concerns reflect a yawning chasm in the profession. How are we to understand these counter-interests? Are they an expression of a pre-postmodernist nostalgia, a turning away and turning back towards a unified humanitarian vision? Or are some of them pointing to possible alternative perspectives? The debate is only beginning to take place.

THE LANGUAGE OF TIME AND SPACE

Lastly, social work has been redirecting its spatio-temporal orientation. Previously, the personal history of the client constituted a central building block in casework or clinical practice, laying the groundwork in an "assessment" phase to social work "interventions." Social work has now refocused its attention towards the present, collapsing its temporal span as indicated by the proliferation of short-term interventions, recently called "brief therapies." The trend is also present in the field of psychology and cuts across theoretical orientations. There are brief versions of psychodynamic therapies, as well as cognitive-behavioural or task-centred interventions. These time-budgeted modalities are consistent with the budgetary constraints on human service organizations, which exert pressures upon social workers to limit the length of time they invest in working with their clients. In hospital environments, short-term planning and discharge are now encouraged in a door-revolving fashion. There is, furthermore, a specific appeal to "solution-focused" therapy, which reinforces this trend. The emphasis on "solutions," vs. the more traditional "problem" orientation, concretizes the move away from "in-depth" understanding (i.e., solutions are to be thought of in the context of deeply rooted problems), to "surface" understanding (i.e., never mind the endless analysis of the past, let's focus on the present and the future).

In a countermove, social work, which was very much bound by its societal conditions of existence to the U.S. and British contexts, is now expanding into the international market of social problems and solutions (in a similar movement to the increased visibility of psychiatry in such international forums as the World Health Organization). The National Association of Social Workers (N.A.S.W.) has recently established a task force on international social work, while its academic counterpart, the Council of Social Work Education is encouraging the development of a new network of academics in this area, as indicated by a recent N.A.S.W. Press title by L. Healy: *Introducing International Development Content in Social Work Curriculum: A Curriculum for Faculty Members in Social Work Programs*, which covers poverty, hunger and development in the global context; rights of the child; domestic and international contexts; and intercountry adoption. In summary, the flattening of client history has coincided with the geographical expansion and "globalization" of the professional venture. These developments are quite consistent with the changing mores of society (i.e., Harvey, 1989).

CHALLENGING NEW DIRECTIONS

Where do we go from here? A critical examination of the language that we use in the social work profession can be incorporated to expand the vision of a reflective social work practice, as suggested by Schon (1987) and earlier by Bloom (1975). This entails questioning the sources and usage of the words we use and understanding their influence in establishing the parameters of social work realities. In our society, in which a quick grasp of condensed words (slogans) and images is being valorized over the development of lengthy arguments (Herman and Chomsky, 1988), what direction can social work take in developing lines of thought and action? Can social workers be expected to accomplish the difficult task of stepping outside of the very institutions of which they are part, as recommended by Mary Douglas (1986), and in the words of Dorothy Smith (1987) consider the "world as problematic?" The words we use categorize the experiences we have as social workers, clients and academics. A similar point was made by Stanley Witkin (1992) who recommended that we re-examine the heuristic value of the questions we raise in our inquiries and the underlying assumptions of the concepts we adopt. In summary, a reflexive orientation would imply the re-examination of the terminology and narratives that constitute our practice as a prevention measure against creeping heteronomy (Bourdieu, 1988).

Specifically, given the loss of a credible metanarrative and the proliferation of fragments of knowledge, we need to reconsider the limitations of adopting a strictly combinatory model or tool-kit approach (Swidler, 1986) in fostering the ongoing development of our knowledge base. In importing multiple frames of reference, we need to recognize the orientations that such combinations of discourse encourage and, conversely, those that they stifle.

On the positive side, the adoption of a critical approach to multiple perspectives in social work may serve as a solid direction of inquiry within which to acknowledge diversity and conflicting interests. Such an orientation can be implemented through a purposeful investigation of the multiple positions that clients, workers and academics occupy in the context of social work activity. I am thinking along the lines of Spivak's (1992) unlayering of the multiple aspects of the self and others (as postcolonial woman, minority, immigrant, academic, etc.), moving us beyond established dichotomies towards greater cognitive complexity, as has been recommended by Berlin (1990) in reference to our modes of inquiry. This direction is thus a rejoinder to Sands and Nuccio, Gorman, and Renaud, and specifically of McBeath and Webb's alternative for a "libertarian/radical view of fragmentation" inspired by Lyotard, as structured plurality, articulating meaning of the fragmentation and redressing imbalance between client and worker.

In the recent years, I have been struck by a trend in doctoral candidates to carve thesis topics which redefine the boundaries of traditional issues —

exploiting fragmentation. These new interests result in a structuration of alternative discourses that challenge traditional dichotomies such as the clinical/ policy arenas. Without taking away the need for rigorous quest, these divisions no longer seem as relevant when we examine the personal/institutional meanings and practices and the internalization of discourses.

Such alternative directions can lay the groundwork for conceptual and empirical explorations, which seem fruitful in gaining an understanding of people's lives and the intertextuality of their discourses, and can provide critical means for drawing from the intertextual knowledge base of the social work profession to open up new horizons of understanding and action.

REFERENCES

Abramson, M. (1985). The autonomy-paternalism dilemma in social work practice. *Social Casework* (Sept): 387–392.

Baudrillard, J. (1983). *Simulations*. New York: Semiotext(e).

Berlin, S. B. (1990). Dichotomous and complex thinking. *Social Service Review* 64(1): 46–59.

Bloom, M. (1975). *The paradox of helping: Introduction to the philosophy of scientific practice*. New York: Wiley.

Bloom, M., K. Wood and A. Chambon. (1991) The six languages of social work. *Social Work* 36(6): 530–534.

Bok, S. (1982). *Secrets: On the ethics of concealment and revelation*. New York: Pantheon Books.

Bourdieu, P. (1988). Vive la crise! For heterodoxy in social science. *Theory and Society* 17(5): 773–787.

Canda, E.R. (1991). East/west philosophical synthesis in transpersonal theory. *Journal of Sociology and Social Welfare* 18(4): 133–152.

Chambon, A. (1993). Stratégies narratives du récit et de la parole: Comment progresse et s'échafaude une méthode d'analyse. *Sociologie et Sociétés* 25(2): 125–135.

Chambon, A., and D. Bellamy. (in press). Ethnic identity, intergroup relations and welfare policy in the Canadian context: A comparative discourse analysis. *Journal of Sociology and Social Welfare*.

Compton, B., and B. Gallaway. (eds.). (1984) *Social work processes. Third edition*. Chicago: The Dorsey Press.

Debord, G. (1967). *La société du spectacle*. Paris: Buchet-Castel.

Douglas, M. (1986). *How institutions think*. Syracuse: Syracuse University Press.

Edelman, M. (1988). *Constructing the political spectacle*. Chicago: The University of Chicago Press.

Foucault, M. (1974) *The archaeology of knowledge*. London: Tavistock.

Gorman, J. (1993). Postmodernism and the conduct of inquiry. *Affilia* 8(3): 247–264.

Halliday, M.A.K. (1973). The syntax enunciates the theme. In *Rules and meanings*, ed. M. Douglas, 279–294. New York: Penguin Books.

Harrison, C., and P. Wood. (1992). *Art in theory, 1900-1990: An anthology of changing ideas*. Cambridge: Blackwell.

Harvey, D. (1989). *The condition of postmodernity*. Cambridge: Blackwell.

Herman, E.S. and N. Chomsky. (1988). *Manufacturing consent: The political economy of the mass media*. New York: Pantheon.

Illich, I. (1978). *Disabling professions*. Boston: M. Boyars.

Imre, R. (1990). Rationality and feeling. *Families in Society* 71: 57–62.

Jameson, F. (1984). Postmodernism or the cultural logic of late capitalism. *New Left Review* 146: 53–92.

McBeath, G.B., and S.A. Webb. (1991). Social work, modernity and postmodernity. *Sociological Review* 39 (Aug/Nov): 745–762.

McMillen, J.C. (1992). Attachment theory and clinical social work. *Clinical Social Work Journal* 20(2): 205–218.

Mirowski, J., C.E. Ross. (1983). Paranoia and the structure of powerlessness. *American Sociological Review* 48: 228–239.

Poster, M., ed. (1988). *Jean Baudrillard: Selected writings*. Stanford: Stanford University Press.

Potter, J., and M. Wetherell. (1987). *Discourse and social psychology: Beyond atttitudes and behaviour*. Newbury Park: Sage.

Reamer, F.G. (1982). *Ethical dilemmas in social service*. New York: Columbia University Press.

Reamer, F.G. (1989). Liability issues in social work supervision. *Social Work* 34(5): 445–448

Renaud, G. (1990). Travail social, crise de la modernité et post-modernité. *Canadian Review of Social Work* 7(1): 27–48.

Ricoeur, P. (1976). *Interpretation theory: Discourse and the surplus of meaning*. Forth Worth, Texas: The Texas Christian University Press.

Rodger, J.J. (1991). Discourse analysis and social relationships in social work. *British Journal of Social Work* 21(1): 63–79.

Sable, P. (1992). Attachment theory: Application to clinical practice with adults. *Clinical Social Work Journal* 20(3): 271–283.

Sands, R.G., and K. Nuccio. (1992). Postmodern feminist theory and social work. *Social Work* 37(6): 489–494.

Schneider, E.L. (1991). Attachment theory and research: Review of the literature. *Clinical Social Work Journal* 19(3): 251-266.

Schon, D.A. (1987). *Educating the reflective practitioner.* San Francisco: Jossey-Bass.

Scott, D. (1989). Meaning construction and social work practice. *Social Service Review* 63(1): 39–51.

Smith, D. (1987). *The everyday world as problematic: A feminist sociology.* Toronto: University of Toronto Press.

Spivak, G. C. (1992). Who claims alterity? In *Art in theory, 1900-1990, An anthology of changing ideas,* eds. C. Hanson and P. Wood, 1119–1124. Cambridge: Blackwell.

Swidler, A. (1986). Culture in action: Symbols and strategies. *American Sociological Review* 51 (April): 273–286.

Turner, F. J. (1986). A multitheory perspective for practice. In *Social work treatment, third edition,* ed. F.J. Turner, 645–658. New York: The Free Press.

Witkin, S.L. (1992). More on questions. *Philosophical Issues in Social Work* 3(2),: 1, 5.